THE GUIDE TO
HUMANE
CRITTER
CONTROL

NATURAL, NONTOXIC PEST SOLUTIONS TO PROTECT YOUR YARD AND GARDEN

THERESA ROONEY

COOL
SPRINGS
PRESS

THIS BOOK IS DEDICATED TO MY MOM, WHO TAUGHT ME
TO LOVE NATURE AND ALL HER CREATURES.

———————

Inspiring | Educating | Creating | Entertaining

Brimming with creative inspiration, how-to projects, and useful information to enrich your everyday life, Quarto Knows is a favorite destination for those pursuing their interests and passions. Visit our site and dig deeper with our books into your area of interest: Quarto Creates, Quarto Cooks, Quarto Homes, Quarto Lives, Quarto Drives, Quarto Explores, Quarto Gifts, or Quarto Kids.

First published in 2017 by Cool Springs Press, an imprint of The Quarto Group, 401 Second Avenue North, Suite 310, Minneapolis, MN 55401 USA. T (612) 344-8100 F (612) 344-8692
www.QuartoKnows.com

Cool Springs Press titles are also available at discount for retail, wholesale, promotional, and bulk purchase. For details, contact the Special Sales Manager by email at specialsales@quarto.com or by mail at The Quarto Group, Attn: Special Sales Manager, 401 Second Avenue North, Suite 310, Minneapolis, MN 55401 USA.

10 9 8 7 6 5 4 3 2 1

ISBN: 978-1-59186-696-1

Digital edition published in 2017   JAN   '18

eISBN: 978-0-7603-5327-1

Library of Congress Cataloging-in-Publication Data

Names: Rooney, Theresa, 1959- author.
Title: The guide to humane critter control : natural and nontoxic solutions
  to protect your yard and garden / Theresa Rooney.
Description: Minneapolis, MN : Cool Springs Press, 2017. | Includes
  bibliographical references and index.
Identifiers: LCCN 2017029501 | ISBN 9781591866961 (sc)
Subjects: LCSH: Garden pests--Control.
Classification: LCC SB603.5 .R66 2017 | DDC 635/.0496--dc23
LC record available at https://lccn.loc.gov/2017029501

Acquiring Editors: Todd Berger, Madeleine Vasaly
Project Manager: Alyssa Bluhm
Art Director: Brad Springer
Cover Designer: Silverglass Design
Layout: Silverglass Design
Illustrations: Bill Kersey

Printed in China

CONTENTS

INTRODUCTION

Every gardener has encountered a pest or two at some time. That pest might simply be annoying or it might threaten an entire crop, a whole growing season, or even the health of the gardener. If you've struggled to keep your yard pest free, this book will give you new concepts and tools to add to your gardening basket and new ways of viewing your outdoor space.

What you will *not* find in these pages is the advice to kill or destroy the pest as a first course of action—the goal here is to deter your pest, mitigate or prevent the damage it may do to your garden, and, if necessary, remove it. Many problems are not truly problems at all; we, sometimes, are our own worst enemy in the yard and garden. As our population grows, we often build in areas that were previously inhabited only by the animals; those animals need somewhere to go and will frequently find a way to live within our urban areas—much to our amazement and sometimes to our dismay. As we remove predators and upset the natural balance we find that some animal and insect populations suddenly increase. These increases are not always pleasant to deal with.

For the home gardener, even a "bad" pest problem is usually not a life-and-death situation for the humans. While losing a crop of tomatoes to tomato hornworms or slugs is monumentally

frustrating, we can learn from our problems and losses and change plant choices or practices. Better than that, of course, is preventing the problems in the first place—and that's exactly what this book will help you do.

We tend to want to regulate and reduce the diversity in our growing spaces so instead of biodiversity in our plantings we have only vast monocultures that attract specific pests or problems. We think that by limiting our plant communities we limit the number of pests and problems but, in reality, we may be increasing our pest problems. Think of those monocultures as an open all-you-can-eat buffet for critters and the biodiverse garden or yard as a tiny portion—hard for a pest to get a full meal.

As a long-time gardener, and someone who simply must know all I can about the world around me, I have studied, observed, and experimented in my garden. I delight in the abundance and diversity in my garden.

Actually, my yard boasts no turf at all. The fruit trees and bushes, herbs, vegetables, flowers for the pollinators, and, yes, weeds fill nearly every nook and cranny. The chickens wander in selected areas at certain times and the urban squirrels seem to have control over the entire yard. I rejoice in finding a new bug or weed or even a new and fascinating fungus. All are a part of the whole and remind me that monocultures can be boring or, at least, an uninteresting place to spend much time.

I hope you find different concepts to consider or new ways to see your garden as a living, breathing, ever-changing whole. Sometimes nature seems out of balance— when the Japanese beetles have attacked every raspberry bush or your precious roses or, perhaps, the ants have built huge hills in your vegetable garden or, once again, the squirrels have ripped out every plant in every newly planted container— but most of these disasters are short lived and the garden and gardener can recover. Relax and take the long view—this is what nature does. We are all in this together— on this tiny blue, green, and white spinning marble in the vastness of space—and we can actually coexist pretty easily with most of what we consider to be pests.

IDENTIFYING PESTS

1

How do you define a pest? It may sound like an obvious question, but the answer depends on what you're growing and your tolerance for disorder or untidiness in your yard and garden. Nature is a messy place—if you desire order and formality, your threshold for pests will be much lower than someone who loves the look of blousy, overgrown gardens, crooked paths, and the evidence of something nibbling on the leaves. Most of us fall somewhere in the middle. There is no right or wrong way to feel; your view is correct for you. Own it and accept all that goes with it.

That said, a pest is simply an unwanted or undesired creature in the garden. It can be an insect, spider, reptile, amphibian, bird, or mammal—even other humans. An animal or insect may be desirable in one person's yard but a pest in another's.

I remind you to think of your outdoor space as a whole. While one plant or potted container may have a pest issue, notice that most of what is growing seems fine. That may help you step back and "take ten" to consider the best approach to your situation—that is, literally, take ten steps back. Can you still see the damage? If not, maybe you can ignore it. This approach may not work in all cases, but it is an option to consider.

Many pests can actually alert you to problems that may be small at the time but that will only get worse. Some pests are not the problem but the secondary "infection"—and what you notice and blame for the entire situation.

Which animals can be pests in your garden? Most of us are familiar with the deer and rabbits that seem to find our gardens delightful, but pests come in all shapes and sizes. Those of us who live in urban or suburban areas are often amazed at the wild animals that inhabit the same space as we do. Some of these animals can be destructive as they search our shared spaces for food. Often, just removing easy sources of food, such as bird feeders, and making sure the garbage is critter proof is all you need to do to convince them to find their sustenance elsewhere.

Those who deal with invasive insects, such as the emerald ash borer or gypsy moth, face tough choices—treat the trees with systemic pesticides and all that entails or remove the trees the pests attack. Sometimes gardeners need to know which insect invaders are on their way and be prepared to deal with them.

And, for those of us with less intimidating but still dangerous pests, we need to remember how to stay safe in nature and keep our yard and gardens free—or as free as they can be—from pests.

As we garden, we know what we want: pretty flowers, healthy vegetables, and green turf. Anything other than that and most of us quickly leap to defend our garden from invaders. Animals of any type are not allowed in. All bugs are bad. Even most birds must be repelled. But that is a narrow view. Many animals can live in our yards and gardens without much impact. Insects are not only wanted but necessary in healthy gardens, and all gardens and yards should support some bird life. Our gardens can withstand all kinds of nibbling and other damage, but it is up to the gardener to determine the limits.

Our yards and gardens will and should attract animals—it is the sign of a healthy ecosystem. Sometimes, though, that system needs corrections. If you are trying to grow a nice green lawn, you don't want grubs to move in and eat all the grass roots, which means your turf dies or your lawn is now home to moles that cause more damage as they rid your lawn of grubs. If you kill the moles or cause them to leave, the grubs are still there destroying the turf. Maybe you opt to kill the grubs—but that could kill all the good bugs and life forms in your lawn; now your lawn suffers as the soil dies and you, as caretaker, must fertilize and water and reseed the lawn to keep it green. So, where do you draw the line? Perhaps a smaller lawn, making sure it is filled with other grasses or clover to minimize the monoculture attraction for the grubs, then making sure there are plenty of birds around to eat the grubs and the beetles that lay the eggs. Other insects and animals will eat the beetles too and help keep their numbers down, but we must allow them access to our lawns. That may mean some temporary damage to enable our lawns to be healthy and strong.

As for the larger pests, such as rabbits or deer, we can usually deter these animals with fencing, by making our gardens a less inviting habitat for them, or by redirecting them to another location in our yard or community. We have destroyed many predators of our pests and can't be surprised when the numbers of rabbits or deer increase. Perhaps if we stop seeing them as pests and, instead, look at them as co-inhabitants in the natural ecosystems we hope to create we will see them in a different light and treat them differently. Nature always works toward a balance, but we humans often do not work in tandem, but against that goal of balance.

Not all pests we encounter are insects or wild animals. Sometimes our pets are the pests. We can easily mitigate the damage they do by realizing what prompted the problem. The same may be said of working with wild animals.

Another pest we may encounter is other humans. Sometimes our neighbors, children, or total strangers may be pests in our yard. Fencing can help, along with lighting, if needed. Strategic plantings work too (see page 38), along with understanding the behavior you have seen.

Recently, after I gave a sustainable-gardening talk, an audience member approached me and asked what pest or animal I thought was eating all his tomatoes—not the cherry or Roma tomatoes, only the regular tomatoes. All the ripe tomatoes were taken at one time and the plants were not damaged. Squirrels were not the cause as no tomatoes were left with only a bite out of them. The plants were grown in containers on a front patio. None of the containers was tipped over as they may have been if raccoons, or even deer, were after them. The culprit? A two-legged pest. Yes, another person. Either a child or adult wanting those ripe tomatoes. No nonhuman animal would have been so neat while taking only the best and ripest fruit. He now knew he needed to protect his harvest from humans too—a tough lesson.

That is not to say, though, that all humans will be pests in your garden. Many gardeners find community in gardening. It brings neighbors together in a wonderful, basic way. We all know what it is like to work hard to create beauty and many of us know how hard it can be to grow our food. That brings us together to watch over each other's gardens and yards and warn each other when we encounter a pest of some kind.

WHAT IS PEST DAMAGE?

This is another question that sounds simple but can be complex to answer. At the most basic level, pest damage is damage caused to your lawn or garden by an animal or insect. But how do you know whether the damage is from pests or a disease or even something else, like the weather? Hail damage can look like insect damage or even a disease. Herbicide damage can look like disease or even vandalism.

If your diagnosis is wrong, your efforts to correct it will be in vain. Be sure of the type of damage you have and its cause before you begin correction. The

If your plants have been pulled out by the roots, deer are most likely to blame.

pages that follow and the table on pages 26 and 27 will help you narrow down the cause(s) of a particular symptom in your plants or lawn.

I admit: I frequently prefer to just let it go. Part of that is my basic laziness but, more, it is because I love to see what happens. I have found that, many times, when I remove my efforts to "correct" the problem, it seems to equalize more quickly. Again, we humans can be an enemy of a healthy lawn and garden.

ASSESSING THE DAMAGE

Let's start by learning how to determine what the problem in our garden really is. Following are some questions to consider.

Have all your plants been affected at the same time? If yes, your garden is most likely experiencing environmental, or even man-made, damage. If everything in your whole yard is wilting, consider: Has the weather been very hot or windy? Simple watering will help.

Do you see damage to one plant only, or a few kinds of plants, perhaps all in one area? Try to narrow the kind of damage you see. If it is to one plant or one kind of plant (all your mint, for example), it may be an insect pest or disease common for that plant. If it is a wider range of plants—the hostas, lilies, and impatiens—the pest problem is more likely an animal, such as a rabbit or deer. The type of damage you see will help determine the culprits.

If your fruit only disappears at the peak of ripeness, it might be an animal pest— but your human neighbors should be considered suspects too.

Where is the damage in your yard? Is it the far gardens? Possibly a larger animal, such as a deer, is enjoying the relative privacy from human intervention. Is the damage under the shrubbery? Look to the rabbits to be nibbling in protected areas. Is the destruction near the front door? Squirrels have little fear and, because we are gone from our homes so frequently, they are justified in knowing we are not much of a threat—or so they think.

What time of day or night does the damage occur? Some animals are active only at night, some only during the evening, and some only during the daytime.

For example, squirrels and chipmunks are usually very active during the day. Rabbits, raccoons, and deer, on the other hand, are usually more active at night or when we are not in our landscapes to see them.

Which plant is damaged? Certain plants attract certain pests. Some plants attract few pests. Some pests love a wide range of plants. Knowing which plant is damaged can help narrow the suspect pool. Many times you will find that your herbs are fine—except for the four-lined plant bugs who seem to enjoy them— whereas young plants, especially hostas and lilies, are nearly irresistible to rabbits and deer. Aphids prefer the soft, green, lush growth of your perennials, while scale will be found safely "hidden" on the bark of your shrubs like magnolia or on your citrus fruit trees that you may be growing in containers. If you plant a vegetable garden, protect the young plants from deer and rabbits. Once the plants have matured a bit and there is more for the deer and rabbits to eat, they may or may not ignore your vegetable garden.

In which part of the growing season do you see the damage? Each insect or animal presents pest damage at certain times of the year. Rabbits are more likely to damage plants in winter when there is little for them to eat, or in early spring while waiting for plants to grow. Insects often prefer tender new growth, so while plants put on lots of growth in early spring the insect population increases to enjoy this additional food. By early summer you may see insect pests and their damage everywhere, but this damage may suddenly slow as insects pupate or come to the end of their life cycle. The caterpillar population peaks in late spring to early summer so it has time to pupate and become butterflies or moths. This is also the time that birds raise their young and need extra protein from caterpillars to feed their babies.

Where on the plant is the damage? Is it only on the top, on the new growth? Only on the bottom, where rabbits can reach it? Only on one side, where the deer can nibble it through the fence?

How long has it been happening? This is where visiting your garden is important. Catching problems early is best. Sometimes we don't see the problem until it is out of control. There may be times you see sudden damage to your plants—overnight, it seems, all the plants on one side of your yard have wilting leaves or branches or are dry and blackened. What you are possibly seeing then is herbicide drift. Somewhere, someone has sprayed an herbicide and the chemical has drifted onto your plants. (For more on herbicide drift, see page 18.)

Do you see any insects? The insects you see may not be the problem, but they may give you hints to the problem's cause. Ants on a plant with wilting leaves may indicate aphids. Wasps and hornets infesting a pine may simply mean the sap is flowing and they are enjoying a meal. Carpenter ants in a tree are not killing the tree but letting you know there is internal rot and it should be evaluated and, perhaps, removed.

Do you see any insect frass (poop) or webbing? Caterpillars and sawflies leave behind lots of black droppings because they eat so much of the leaves in one area of the plant. Spiderwebs are a great thing to find—they mean your yard is healthy and the spiders are enjoying the insects you may call pests. Spider mite webbing, very tiny and often hard to see, is another story; these tiny sucking insects will suck the life from your plants.

And finally, what type of damage do you see? Is the whole plant being eaten? Leaves and stems? Probably an animal. Only the leaves? Possibly an insect. Has something damaged the plant, but the plant is still there? Possibly environmental damage, disease, or a small insect, such as a mite or scale or aphid, is the cause. The information that follows will help you match the damage to the cause.

When a plant is hit by a boring insect, its limbs wilt only past the point of entry.

Wilting

Are all your plants wilting, but you know you've had enough rain that dehydration shouldn't be an issue?

If your lawn and garden endure a storm or a flood, you can detect this damage easily. Everyone on the block may have the same issues. All yards may show bushes bent over, trees toppled, or perennials bent to the ground. This makes your "pest" problem pretty easy to figure out. Mother Nature has affected your outdoor space in a not-so-pleasant way. Plant roots need to breathe, so if they are under water for any period of time they die. This means, then, the aboveground part of the plant will wilt—the roots are no longer able to sustain it. So, even plants in waterlogged soil can wilt. To save the plants you must get the soil to dry out before all the roots are dead. Sometimes this is not possible and you will have to start over. Sometimes you can pull back the mulch so the sunshine and winds dry the soil and your plants will recover. If you have heavy clay soil, consider planting your plants a bit higher—with the crown at or slightly above soil level so water drains away. Don't overwater if your soils are heavy.

Borers or boring insects damage your plants by causing leaves or branches to start to wilt past the point of their entry. Their boring into the stems and limbs of your plants blocks nutrients and water from being transported from the leaves to the roots and vice versa. The outermost end of the stem or limb starts to wilt and die. If you see this early, you can often prevent more damage. If you wait too long, the limb, or even the plant itself, may die. Borers are an issue you need to deal with, as they kill limbs, branches, and, sometimes, entire plants or trees. The emerald ash borer is a beautiful tiny green insect that destroys entire forests and city-forests of ash trees. Often, borers prefer one plant or family of plants, so just knowing which plant is affected gives you an idea of the possible cause.

Broken Branches, Nibbled Leaves, and Uprooted Plants

If a number of plants, or even shrubs or trees, are tipped completely over, it's probably due to a windstorm—it could be a straight-line wind, tornado, or hurricane.

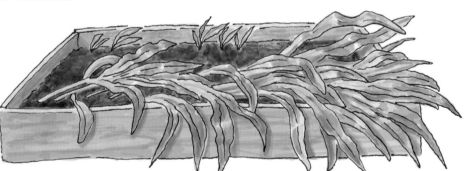

Were all your plants damaged at once? Storm damage is a more likely culprit than critters, or it's possible that a rabbit or deer laid on them at night.

Plants that are bitten off close to the ground at a sharp 45-degree angle (left) are usually the work of rabbits. If the bites are more ragged and 10 inches or so of the plant is left (right), you're most likely dealing with deer.

What if a number of branches from many shrubs are broken and many leaves from a wide variety of plants are torn or look like they have been chewed off? If you work outside the home or are away on vacation, you don't really know what goes on in your yard during the day. This type of damage may mean your garden was hit by hail while you were gone.

Next, think about the time of year or part of the growing season you see the damage. In midwinter, many pests are sleeping or hibernating, so the gallery of choices is smaller. In midsummer, rabbits likely won't bother your plants as they enjoy the clover you planted in the lawn or are happily nibbling on new tender weeds rather than your established lilies. But come midwinter, those same rabbits will inflict devastation on your dormant roses, spirea, or even the newly planted apple tree. There is just nothing else for them to eat.

Identify which plant has been eaten or pulled out. Were the bean plants pulled out by their roots or just nibbled down to a height of about 10 inches? In both cases, deer are probably the guilty party.

Rabbits and mice will girdle your tree trunks, eating the bark all the way around, especially in winter. If left unchecked, this can kill the trees.

Are the branches cut off in a rough or ragged manner about 2 feet off the ground or higher? Browsing deer will damage shrubs as they pull off the tender leaves. Are the plant stems cut off sharply at 45-degree angles? Rabbits have sharp teeth and make clean cuts as they remove branches and stems. And they often eat the stems to, or nearly to, the ground.

Damaged or Missing Fruit

Checking on your edible garden, you find black marks all over many of your fruits, like apples, or your tomatoes or peppers, which looked fine until they started to ripen. The marks may appear at the top of each fruit or all on one side. Again, your plants may have been damaged by hail, which bruises the fruit, and this damage takes time to appear. While it may look like insect or even bird damage, such damage over a wide area, or affecting numerous kinds of plants, implies an environmental issue, not a bird or insect problem. Pick the fruit, eat it quickly, and enjoy it fresh. Don't can or preserve this fruit, as it is not perfect. Most of the problems described so far have been ones we can blame on Mother Nature or on humans.

Environmental damage and herbicide drift are problems you can't control—unless you are the one using the herbicide. Herbicide drift happens when the herbicide is used incorrectly—for example, when it is windy, or even when the temperature is too hot or cold. When this happens, the chemical does not fully stay where it is sprayed, instead floating on the wind or evaporating and then condensing somewhere else. When this happens, it can injure or even kill plants that were not the intended targets. If you notice sudden wilting of your plants—say, all on one side of the yard or all on one side of the plants—and multiple varieties and species are affected, you may be dealing with herbicide drift. All you can do is to remove

It's easy to mistake hail-related bruising for bird or insect damage at first glance. If the black spots are mostly on the tops and sides of the fruit and have affected a wide swath of plants all at once, it's the storm.

anything that has died and treat the plant gently as it recovers. Make sure it gets watered if needed, and don't fertilize it. If you know the herbicide drift is very recent (within an hour or two), you can try spraying water on the plants to wash off the chemicals. Usually though, we don't know until we see the resulting damage. If you have ruled out these causes, other pests may be the problem.

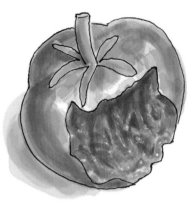

Thirsty squirrels like to eat part of a tomato, abandoning the rest on your lawn. Placing a water source in your yard helps head this off.

Sticky Leaves

Sucking insects, such as aphids, suck their food in liquid form directly from the plants, usually from the soft stems not protected by heavy bark. This liquid is filled with many nutrients and also sugars. As the insects suck, they excrete excess sugars and moisture. This "honeydew" then falls onto lower leaves and stems and even the ground. If you notice sticky plant leaves—like someone poured honey over them—it is this honeydew. This sweet honeydew is one reason ants can be found on plants with aphids. The ants actually "milk" the aphids for their honeydew, stroking the aphids and gathering the sweet extra sugars that they are excreting. The ants drink this as it is high in energy. They also protect that plant from insects that would eat the aphids. So, if you see ants climbing all over a plant, that may be the reason. Many ants also enjoy a bit of nectar from many flowers, which is why you may see ants on peonies.

White Substance on Leaves

Sometimes diseases or fungus and mold can be mistaken for a pest problem. Diseases usually happen to the same plants at the same time each year during the same conditions. Are your leaves covered with a white powdery substance? This is powdery mildew. Many plants are susceptible to it. It looks like your plants have been dusted with talcum

Honeydew

powder. If you spray the plants with water the
mildew is killed and washed off. But, if the same
conditions continue—hot, humid weather, heavy
dew, or plants that don't get enough air circulation—
the mildew will return. Powdery mildew is common
on lilac, *Monarda* (bee balm), squash, and pumpkins.

White fluffy film thicker than powdery mildew
is *downy* mildew. If you see white cotton-like bits
in the leaf axils (where the leaves join the stem or
under the leaves) those are mealybugs. Mealybugs can
also be found on the leaves—they will look like fuzzy cotton.

Powdery mildew

Do you have black spots that appear and grow larger or start to turn dead
or brown in the center of the spots? This is probably a fungal disease—it differs
from insect damage in that the spots grow in size rather than multiply in
numbers like they may for insect damage. The spots often have a halo of lighter
green or yellow around them, but not always.

Molded honeydew

Blackened Leaves

Are all, or many, leaves on a number of different plants, trees, or shrubs
suddenly black or brown, curling, or deformed? Perhaps all on one
side of the shrubs or at the tops? If yes, look to something like an
herbicide drift. Herbicides kill plants. If not used properly, the active
ingredient can drift on the winds and, sometimes, the drifting distance
can be as many as 3 to 5 miles away. Many times, a brush with
an herbicide can knock your plants back, but they may recover.
Direct contact with many herbicides may be deadly to many
plants. It all depends on how much poison the plant experiences.

Your first thought on seeing black leaves may be they are
dead from disease or that those twisted or disfigured leaves have
been hit by an herbicide drift or disease. In reality, though, they are
having their very lives sucked out of them by aphids. If you haven't

Questions to Ask When the Pest Is Larger Than an Insect

- At what time of year is the damage seen?
- Are you seeing holes dug in the lawn? Under a plant or near a foundation?
- How large are the holes and how many are there? A few large ones? Many small (under 3") holes over a wide area?
- Are the holes in the garden?
- What plant, or part of the plant, is damaged?
- What kind of damage is it? Removal of part or all of the plant? Destruction? Are the plants or seeds or containers dug up? Do you see evidence of gnawing or chewing, or do you see holes in the leaves?
- At what time of day or night does the damage occur?
- Where in your yard is this happening? Open space, protected area, specific garden, or the lawn?
- Has this happened before?
- Do other yards show the same kind of damage?
- What else has changed from the past season when you did not have this damage? Different precipitation/heat/storms? Has the area changed? New homes? Removal of homes? New families with different pets that may affect wild animals?

visited the plants in a while and don't catch the early warning signs of an infestation, the honeydew (see page 19) actually starts to mold. This mold often turns black and may cause your plant's leaves to look black or even the ground under the plant to be covered in this black mold. Sometime the leaves become disfigured or twisted from the insects' feeding.

Are you finding black mold only on the tops of the leaves (not the underside) or only on the lower level, or scaffolding, of leaves? If you look at your tomato plant you will see that the leaves grow in levels, older leaves are the lower levels and as the plant grows more levels are added. Think of the floors in a building; the plant grows leaves much like this, or twisted or disfigured leaves mainly on one branch or near the tips of several branches, as the result of aphid feeding. Look for aphids, those soft-bodied insects usually found on the underside of leaves or on the plant's soft stems.

Scale insects may also produce some of this damage, but they are usually concentrated on the stems so the resulting damage would be leaf/branch wilt and dieback.

Black Spots

Insects with scraping mouthparts actually scrape off just layers of leaves. Four-lined plant bugs create perfect pinhead-sized scraped circular areas on the leaves they eat. These marks often turn black as the tissue dies and it looks like the leaves have tiny black circles all over them. The circles sometimes blend together into large marked areas.

Rose slugs, which are not slugs at all but sawfly larvae, enjoy scraping off the layers of rose leaves. Often, they start at the bottom of the plant and work their way up. They leave behind brown sections of leaves that look see-through. Usually they work between the veins in the leaves so the brown stained-glass look is very angular.

When you see various leaves on the plant with marks on them try to distinguish a pattern. Where is the damage? Top of the plant? Tender new leaves? Bottom of the plant where the rose slugs crawl and hide from predators?

When looking at the damage, just look—really look. Many insect pests are extremely well camouflaged—those

Damage from four-lined plant bugs

Damage from leaf-cutter ants or bees

rose slugs and other sawfly larvae often are an exact shade of green to match the plants they are on. I often tell people the damage they saw was from rose slugs and they don't believe me. How could they miss those wormy, caterpillar-like insects? Then they look, really look, and suddenly see their poor rosebush is covered with them. You don't see them until you see them.

Or perhaps, like the four-lined plant bug, the pests are fast movers and hide when you walk by. But as soon as they think it is safe, they pop out from under and behind the leaves to resume their dining on your precious mint (*Mentha*) or *Rudbeckia.*

Chewed Edges

Insects that eat the plant's leaves may take bites from all around the edges or from the center. One really cool kind of "bite" I personally love to see is the perfect half-round circles cut from the leaves' edges. Every time I see this I know those leaf-cutter bees and leaf-cutter ants have grabbed some of the leaf to line their homes—a perfect "wallpaper" for them and one I am glad to supply for my pollinating and other insect helpers. Instead of seeing this as damage, I look at it as more leaf texture and shape! If, however, you see partially eaten or skeletonized leaves, you have an issue to deal with.

Skeletonized Leaves

Skeletonized leaves look like skeletons of leaves, only the ribs or veins remain because the rest of the tissue has been eaten. Caterpillars and beetles often eat sections of leaves or entire leaves. Unless the plants are losing all, or at least half, their leaves it may not be something to worry about.

Skeletonized leaves

Remember that "step back plan" (page 9)? Plants grow lots of extra leaves for just this purpose—for insects or animals to eat. It is all part of the plan. Yes, they need the leaves for photosynthesis, and every leaf lost affects their ability to provide nutrition for themselves, but with so many leaves they actually can afford to lose some. They do this so leaf-eating insects are attracted in sufficient numbers to feed the birds and other insectivores who then may provide other benefits to the plants in addition to pest control, such as fertilization, pollination, pruning, or seed dispersal. Isn't it amazing how intricate the plan is?

Brown Trails

Leafminers are other insects you may encounter. They leave behind brown meandering trails in the leaves. Columbines are notorious targets for

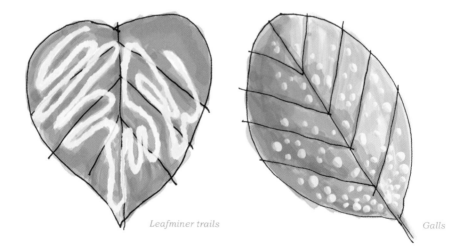

Leafminer trails   *Galls*

leafminers, as they have tender early leaves and the miners are active early in the growing season. You will also find that cabbage, kale, even spinach may be affected—again, these plants put on lots of new growth very early in the growing season and have tender leaves. These soft leaves are perfect places for the miners to live and eat their way through the leaf tissue. The trails usually just mark the leaves and are generally not a health issue for the plant—there is usually lots of healthy green leaf left to photosynthesize. If you don't like the look, remove the leaves and toss them in the compost. By the time you notice them, the miners may have already left. Usually, the perennial plant will regrow enough leaves during the rest of the season, past the time of infestation, and recover just fine. In addition, like every other "damage" that bothers the gardener, once removed the plant looks healthier and the gardener feels better.

Quick Guide: Questions to Ask

- **Which plant is damaged?**
- **In which part of the growing season do you see the damage?**
- **Where on the plant is the damage?**
- **What kind of damage is it?**
- **How long has it been happening?**
- **Do you see any insects?**
- **Do you see any insect frass? Webbing?**
- **Do you see increased insect activity? Ants? Wasps? Ladybugs? Lacewings? Praying mantis?**

DECODING COMMON GARDEN PROBLEMS

PART AFFECTED	SYMPTOM	CULPRIT
Leaves	Leaves are falling all over your yard, it is not autumn, and the fallen leaves are green and, often, even small branches.	Squirrels—they are clearing the branches to allow better movement through their territory
	Leaves have holes in them, not caused by hail.	Beetles, caterpillars, slugs
	Leaves have parts missing on the edges, like they are being eaten.	Leaf-cutter bees or ants, caterpillars, even birds
	Leaves are skeletonized—only veins remain.	Beetles, rose slugs, sawfly larva
	Leaves have black/brown dots on them, about the size of a pinhead.	Four-lined plant bug
	Leaves have silvery or shiny trails on them and perhaps also holes.	Slugs
	Yellowing	Perhaps aphids, mealybugs, scale, or whitefly
		Leaves damaged by heavy winds and partially broken from the branch may yellow and wilt.
		Leaves at the bottom of a plant may yellow because they are old or they are not getting enough sun. If the rest of the plant is healthy in this case, don't worry.
	Leaves have fluffy white cottony "things" on them.	Mealybugs
	Leaves have brown trails in them, like they were drawn with a marker or paint.	Leafminer
	Leaves are sticky—like they are covered with honey or glue.	Aphids (you are seeing honeydew)
	Leaves are wilting but no branch is broken and no borer is found.	Aphids, mealybugs, scale, or other sucking insects
	Leaves are black like they are moldy.	Aphids, and the honeydew has molded
	Lots of black speckles of "something" on the plant and the leaves may be partially or total eaten.	Caterpillar, beetle, or sawfly larva; the black speckled stuff is insect frass (insect poop).
	Webbing on leaves or branches	Armyworms and/or bagworms (leaves will be eaten), spider mites (leaves will be wilting or yellowing), or real spiders (arachnids)—cheer! These are the good guys. Tent caterpillars or bagworms hang out inside the webbing and look like caterpillars.
	Leaves have bumps on them, any shape or size, on top or bottom; not all leaves may be impacted.	Galls: These are either insect egg cases or the result of insect feeding. Nothing to worry about. They look weird or scary but your plants don't mind them. As long as the leaves are mostly green your plant or tree is fine. Think of it as extra leaf texture or interest.
	Hot pink color on leaves that should not be that color	Eriophyid mites; not really a big deal. Consider it interesting color for the plant that year.
	Brown marks between the veins of the leaves	Rose slug or some other insect with a scraping mouthpart taking only the top layer off; look at the specific plant to see which insects prefer it. Some diseases may appear like this. If the patches get bigger it could be disease; if they seem to multiply, probably insects.
	White fluffy stuff on leaves	White, thicker film than powdery mildew is downy mildew. If you see white cotton-like bits in the leaf axils—where the leaves join the stem or under the leaves—those are mealybugs.

PART AFFECTED	SYMPTOM	CULPRIT
	White powdery look to the leaves	Powdery mildew
	Black spots appear and grow larger or start to die or turn brown in the center of the spots.	Probably a fungal disease—it differs from insect damage in that the spots grow in size rather than multiply in numbers as they may for insect damage. The spots often have a "halo" of lighter green or yellow around them, but not always.
Branches	Branches broken off at sharp angles, perhaps eaten or left—usually at 2' or less from the ground	Rabbits—hungry or just nibbling on your plants
	Branches broken off and the ends appear ragged or frayed, can be up to 6' from the ground	Deer—they are not as neat as rabbits
	Arborvitae small branches pruned off the plants anywhere on the shrub/tree	Squirrels—probably looking for nesting material
	One branch or one limb suddenly has wilting leaves	Disease (depends on tree/shrub), more likely borer insect; could also be a result of physical damage by you, animals climbing in the tree, the dog running into the shrub, or kids tossing balls in the bushes or falling into the bushes while they play. The broken branches will start to wilt.
Whole Plant	Plants pulled out from newly planted containers or just-planted garden beds and left on the ground	Squirrels—busy seeing what was planted/buried in their territory
	Plants pulled up from the ground and eaten partially, or they are missing	Deer—they were hungry, or possibly a human thief
	Plants nibbled to the ground as soon as they appear	Rabbits. This is especially a problem in early spring or with baby bunnies.
Ground/Lawn	All seeds planted in the vegetable garden are gone.	Birds, most likely, but ants will take seeds, as will squirrels or chipmunks
	Holes in the lawn or compost pile, may be 3" deep or more, sporadic placement	Squirrel, looking to bury or retrieve food
	Holes dug in the lawn or compost about 1" to 2" wide	Skunk, opossum, raccoon, or armadillo looking for and finding grubs in the lawn
	Organized holes drilled into the trunk or branch of a tree, often in lines	Probably a bird—sapsucker looking for insects and sap
	Many holes drilled in the trunk or branch of a tree, may be more random in spacing	Woodpecker—probably looking for insects
	D-shaped holes in the tree trunk—not a lot of them, maybe only a few	Bronze birch borer, emerald ash borer, or other borers; depends on the tree and the damage you see
Fruit	All your nearly ripe tomatoes, peppers, or other harvest are suddenly gone	Probably another human
	All your fruit from the trees is suddenly gone	Humans may steal the entire harvest at one time; squirrels or birds take one piece of fruit or berry at a time.
Trunk/Bark	The bark around the base/bottom of a tree or shrub is stripped away or missing. Branches also may be bare of bark.	Probably rabbit damage during winter—they had to eat something. Mice will also do some damage. When this encircles an entire tree trunk it is called "girdling."
	Similar damage as previous, only higher up—more than 3' above any snow fall line	Deer—they were hungry during the winter
Other	Lots of ants on the tree or plant	Decaying trees are great places for ants to live; if you see lots of ants on a plant, look for aphids being farmed or milked by the ants.

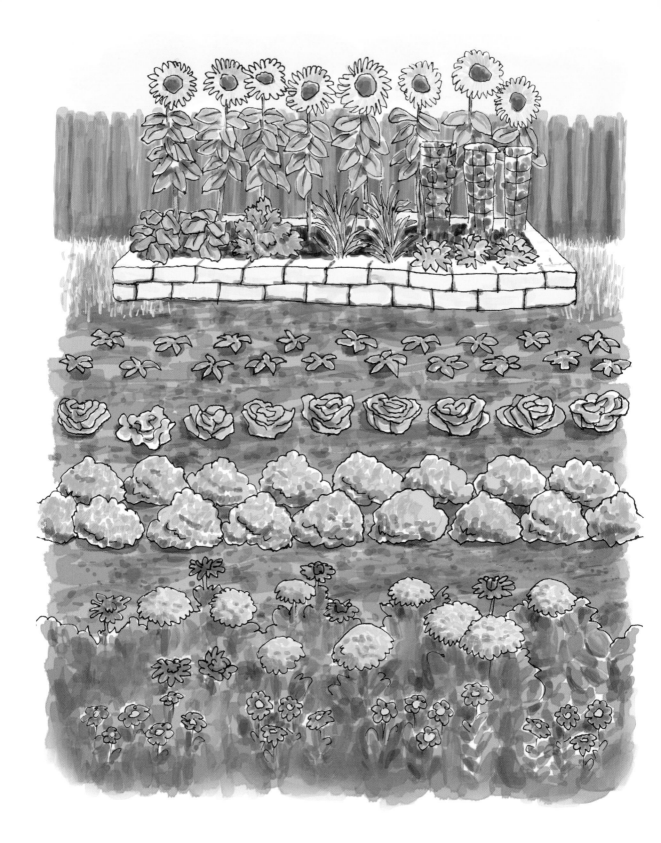

A HEALTHY GARDEN REPELS PESTS

2

Pick up any gardening magazine or follow any gardening blog and you'll find a hundred different ways to landscape your yard and gardens. Theories abound concerning colors and bloom times and heights of plants. What is the look you want in your garden? Do you want to grow only native plants? Is the turf your pride and joy? Do you have children or pets? Do you want to grow vegetables or fruit or herbs? These are only a few of the design elements you may find featured in any article.

Dandelions are considered weeds by many people, but their deep taproots are good for the soil and their flowers are beneficial to bees.

Research online and you will find more opinions about the best plants or the best way to garden than there may be varieties of plants—well, almost. The possibilities are endless and it can be overwhelming to the novice gardener and, even, to a long-time seasoned gardener.

This chapter talks about what makes a healthy garden and how to begin. There are many questions meant to spark ideas to consider or inspire you. Write them down, think about them, and start gardening. It is so much easier to change plans on paper than it is to dig up and move all your plants.

Before we get into the specifics that will help you grow a healthier landscape, let me share with you one action that can really help the lawn and garden caretaker: visit your lawn or garden every day. I like to think our plants enjoy it when we visit, but it is to our benefit to do so. By visiting your landscape each day, you get to appreciate the beauty you are creating and be inspired by it. We know nature can improve our mental and, even, physical health, but you can also improve your landscape's health with frequent visits.

There is a saying, "The best fertilizer for a garden is the gardener's shadow." Our landscape does better when we pay attention to it—and isn't that one reason you created your beautiful landscape? Take the time to visit your garden each day. Make it part of your schedule. Let someone else do the dishes or give the children a bath while you spend some time keeping the lawn and garden looking good. Consider this my free pass to use with your family to get some lawn or garden time. It is required. You are welcome.

Seeing your plants every day of the growing season helps you spot trouble easily when it starts. One of the first lessons gardeners can learn is to anticipate the water needs of your plants. You may only see them when they start to droop, but the next time you may notice the plants look less "happy," less "shiny," or not as "glossy." Then the next day they show signs of wilting. By recognizing this connection, you realize their lackluster appearance signals an impending moisture shortage.

Seeing them every day also means you can spot trouble from pests much more quickly—often before it becomes a big deal. Unhealthy plants will attract many insect pests. Just as we humans seem to succumb to colds when we feel run down, our plants also seem to be hit more frequently from some insect pests when they are not as healthy as they could be. When your plants continually deal with wilting and being revived, they become stressed. And, of course, the wrong plant in the wrong place will stress the plant too (and the gardener). I discuss more gardening ideas in the next chapter to grow a healthier garden.

BOOST YOUR GARDEN'S IMMUNE SYSTEM

You likely already know that the best defense is a good offense. Well the best defense for your garden's protection is to create a healthy ecosystem in your yard and garden. So, take the offense: Take the initiative to make your garden as healthy as you possibly can. And healthy outdoor spaces rebound more quickly from pest problems. You don't have to start from scratch. Make changes as you are able and soon you will see the changes increase the health of your garden. As these changes take hold you'll also realize that your garden is easier to care for, freeing up more time for even more changes if you wish.

Healthy plants combat insect and disease pests much more easily. If your garden is healthy, with fewer "bad" bugs around—such as Japanese beetles or grubs in the lawn—there will be fewer insects to attract pests such as skunks or raccoons, or even opossums, looking for those tasty morsels. Birds will flock to your healthy outdoor space and make short work of many insect pests that may plague your plants.

All plants need a certain amount of sunshine. Full-sun plants need six to eight hours of sun a day and that includes the hot midday sun. Part-sun plants can thrive with less sun, maybe four to six hours and no hot midday sun. Shade plants usually get little or no direct sun, but they must have some indirect light. If you can't read a book because the area is too dark, it is too dark for your plants.

Soil is the most important part of a healthy lawn and garden, and most plants like moist, well-drained soil rich with organic material. How healthy are your plants? If they seem to be fairly healthy, your soil drains after a rain but does not need continuous watering between rains, and you don't need to apply lots of fertilizers to keep your plants healthy, your soil is probably fine. If, however, you find that your soil stays very wet after a rain for a long time (a common problem with clay soils) or if you need to water soon after a rain and frequently after that (as tends to happen with sandy soils), then your garden would most likely benefit from the addition of more organic matter, such as compost.

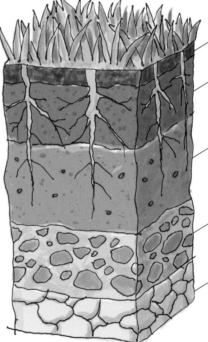

Humus—decomposing organic material

Topsoil—a mix of humus and minerals

Eluviation layer—mostly sand and silt; minerals, clay, and nutrients have been leached from it

Subsoil—where the leached materials wind up, including clay and minerals

Bedrock—broken and unbroken rocks; plant roots do not usually go down this far

Soil is much more than the layer you see on the surface.

If you have been using a lot of synthetic fertilizers in your landscape, you may notice that the soil is not as healthy; most of these fertilizers do contain salts and other chemicals that will impact the natural life in the soil. As you wean your landscape off synthetic fertilizers to more organic types, it is natural that you may see more weeds or encounter growing problems until the soil health is renewed. At that time, however, you should then see that your landscape suddenly becomes much healthier with much fewer inputs from you. Because few of us have this wonderfully organic soil naturally in our yards we should consider amending our soils with compost whenever we can. A few plants, such as nasturtiums and wisteria, prefer a very lean soil—one not so rich—so go easy on the added compost or manures for these plants. Even our native perennials and most of our ornamental perennials do best with a healthy soil and not much extra fertilizer added by the gardener. Compost for these perennials is welcome.

If your soil is very sandy, compost will help it hold water and nutrients. If you have heavy clay soil, compost will help break up the soil structure and allow water to move more freely. If your soil has low fertility—few readily available nutrients for the plants—compost will increase it. Sometimes you may have a soil that has nutrients in it, but they are not available to the plants because the bacteria, fungi, and other soil life are not present to work with the plants to access the nutrients. It is a wonderfully complex web of life under our feet. If your soil is compacted or being eroded, compost will help with those issues as well. Do you sense a theme? Compost may be the answer to many garden problems.

Whenever you start a new garden or redo a lawn, consider having a soil test done by your local extension office or university. These tests will tell you much about your soil and will often come with specific recommendations on how to correct any problems as well. What is its pH (is it alkaline or acid)? How much organic matter does your soil have? Certain bacteria and fungi and other soil life thrive at different pH levels, and these work with your plants to access the nutrients in the soil and in the plant. If your plant requires a low pH—as is the case with azaleas or blueberries—and the pH of your soil is too high, the soil life the plants need to access the nutrients will not be present, and the plant will struggle and perhaps die. If you correct the pH or grow plants that do best at the pH your soil has you will see better results. Compost will not impact pH very much, if at all, so you will need to make these corrections through other means. Contact your local extension office on the best way for you to do that if you need to. What is the structure of your soil (sandy, clay, loam)? Plant roots need both air and water. If your soil allows the water to filter through too quickly, your plants may not be able to make sufficient use of it. The nutrients too will leach out quickly in these sandy soils. Heavy clay soils, on the other hand, have little space between the soil particles for air that the roots need, and often what little space exists gets filled up with water—then the roots may die, as they can't access any air. Clay soils often are rich soils, but they may be so waterlogged that the soil life can't exist there or they may be come dry and compacted and repel water so even water is not available to the plant roots. Again, compost will help to mitigate both soil types. clay and sandy.

Healthy soil is the basis for your healthy yard and garden. If the soil is not healthy you will never have a healthy garden. If your garden is not healthy, you will see more insect pest damage and more diseases in your plants. If your garden is not healthy, the damage caused by bigger pests, such as deer or rabbits or even armadillos, will be more pronounced and your garden may not recover, or recover much more slowly. Healthy gardens go a long way to keeping pests at bay or minimizing their impact.

GROW NATIVE

Choosing plants native to your area is a great way to find something that grows happily in your climate without too much work. One of the best places to find plant selections and suggestions for your area is your local extension office. You need to learn what gardening zone or heat zone you live in.

The US Department of Agriculture created a map of zones for gardeners. This is the USDA Plant Hardiness Zone Map. The farther north you are, the smaller the number for your zone. People along the Canadian border may live in zones 2, 3, or even 5, depending upon temperatures during hot summers and the below-zero winters.

The No-Dig Garden

No-dig gardening is a way to improve your soil without digging up your garden. Follow these steps:

1. Cut down whatever vegetation is there—weeds, grass, etc. Leave the cut foliage right there, as it will compost under the next layers.

2. Water the soil well.

3. Cover the entire area with newspaper—use 5 to 10 sheets for this layer if normal weeds are present. If hardy weeds such as thistle, creeping Charlie, kudzu, or others are there, use 20 or more sheets of newspaper, or even cardboard or cotton or wool carpet. The tougher/stronger weeds may escape from under or between your paper or cardboard layer, so make sure you overlap them well and watch for reemerging weeds. Water this layer well.

4. Cover it with compost, dried leaves, or mulch. Water this top layer well too. You are ready to plant now or wait a season to plant.

Aside from saving you a lot of hard work, by not digging up the entire garden area you do not disturb the soil bacteria and fungi and do not bring weed seeds to the surface to sprout. The current bacteria and fungi will help keep your soil healthy and your plants happy. And, because most weed seeds need light to germinate they will not germinate under the newspapers, compost, or mulch you placed on top. It is important to water each layer well as it starts the decomposition and composting of the layers (which adds nutrition and organic matter to the soil) and also keeps the moisture level up until those layers break down enough to let the rain reach the soil again.

Because you are not disturbing the soil, there will be fewer weed seeds exposed to attract any birds or other pests and the plants will establish quickly so they don't attract insect pests. The lack of

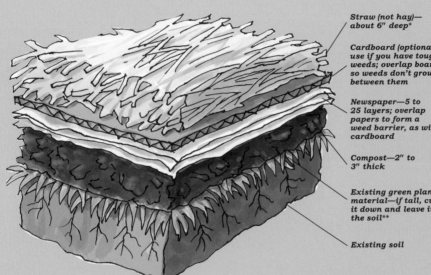

Straw (not hay)—about 6" deep*

Cardboard (optional)—use if you have tough weeds; overlap boards so weeds don't grow between them

Newspaper—5 to 25 layers; overlap papers to form a weed barrier, as with cardboard

Compost—2" to 3" thick

Existing green plant material—if tall, cut it down and leave it on the soil**

Existing soil

*Water each layer well before adding the next layer.

**If you are dealing with buckthorn or black walnut, remove as much material as possible. Both plants contain chemicals that inhibit or even kill other plants. You want to remove as much of them as you can.

freshly disturbed soil will allow the squirrels to continue in the area without lots of digging where you have dug.

If you want to plant right away, pull back the compost or mulch, punch a hole in the paper, and dig into the soil. Plant the plant as you normally would in the correctly sized hole and amend the backfill soil with a bit of compost. Water the plant in well. The newspaper acts as a barrier against the weeds and yet will decompose after about one growing season. Cardboard lasts a bit longer so take that into consideration with your plantings. They may need a bit more watering until the cardboard breaks down enough to let water filter through to the growing roots.

To build even more organic levels look into "lasagna" gardening. Layer straw, compost, leaves, etc., 1 foot high or even higher to create a wonderfully rich and dynamic growing substrate for your plants.

The American Horticultural Society developed the AHS Plant Heat Zone Map, which takes into consideration many factors, including the number of days above 86°F. With the Plant Heat Zone Map, higher-numbered zones are hotter. As our climate changes, the zone you live in may change. Plants are affected by cold and heat, as are the pests. Think about the changes your yard and garden may see over the next twenty, or fifty, years and take that into consideration when planting. For example, where I live pines still do well, but in thirty years or so the climate here may not be as conducive to growing pines. In that case, the trees will then be more susceptible to new pests or diseases. I need to consider that the pine I plant today may be shorter lived than those planted fifty years ago. If I plant that pine, I need to be aware it may attract more pests now than it may have twenty years ago.

Future climactic conditions are a bit tough for the average gardener to anticipate, but do consider that your garden may begin to see more heavy rain events (2 inches or more in one storm) or stronger straight-line winds. These winds can be very destructive; almost as much as more major storms, like hurricanes or tornadoes. Your garden may also see more flooding if you live in an area that is currently prone to flooding; even if your area has never flooded you may want to consider that it could happen. Another impact to consider

This is an alternative to lasagna gardening on page 35. Water each layer well before adding the next one.

Compost—2" thick

Newspaper—5 to 25 layers thick; add more layers when dealing with tougher weeds

Compost—2" thick

Soil

If you have a persistent deer problem, choose ornamental grasses and other plants they aren't attracted to for the less-protected areas of your yard.

when planting is because we will be experiencing more hot, dry times during our summers, your landscape may be impacted by fires. If you live in a fire prone area this is something to consider as you choose your plant materials. An easy way to think about future problems is to think about the minor problems you are seeing now—not enough water? Too much water? Too much wind? And then consider that those minor problems will soon become the normal experience for your garden. Whatever conditions you and your garden are experiencing will be more intense.

As our growing seasons become longer some of the pests that we have encountered only infrequently may become more regular visitors to our yards. Our winters may be milder and this means that the pests that would have normally been killed off will survive over the winter. The cold, brutal winters that may have culled our urban rabbit populations are now so mild that nearly all the rabbits survive the winter and the breeding population in the spring is much larger, resulting in even more rabbit pressure on our landscapes. The same is happening with the whitetail deer populations. Japanese beetles are moving into areas that have never experienced them before.

Keep hostas and other "deer candy" closer to your house, where the animals are less likely to venture.

Climate is not the only pest mover, people move pests from location to location by moving firewood, wooden pallets, plant materials, and even just by the fact that we move from area to area, we may bring pests with us. So, we need to be aware of the possible future problems we may see. Of course, we can't know for sure what will happen but as a gardener just start being aware of what could be coming to your yard soon.

Another resource for what works in your area, and what doesn't, is your local horticulture or garden club or group. They will have lots of experiences and tips they can share with you. Again, there is no right or wrong way to put in your garden as long as you enjoy it, the right plants are in the right place, and you can keep up with it.

Okay, you know the garden should be healthy, but how does that help with pest issues? I have mentioned a few in passing and following are more ways your healthy outdoor space can be less pest filled.

PLANT STRATEGICALLY

When choosing what to plant in your yard, consider the pests common to your area. If you live where there is a large deer population, it makes little sense to plant wide swaths of hosta, which is like deer candy. If you, instead, choose ornamental grasses and herbs to plant in the sunshine and plants such as turtlehead, columbine, coralbells, bleeding hearts, epimediums, ferns, and native ephemeral plants the deer will not be attracted to your yard. You may also encounter less slug damage and have a much more interesting and vibrant shade garden.

When you plant your outdoor space thickly, using all the layers, filling them with plants many times, there is no space for deer or rabbits, both of which need a little open space like the edge of a meadow or open field to feel comfortable. Fewer open spots may mean fewer small plants for the rabbits to eat in spring. The deer won't wander into your yard if they can't see enough open areas to make sure predators are not lurking, waiting to attack. The rabbits like to hide under shrubs, but if those shrubs are underplanted with fragrant herbs the rabbits won't want to be there.

If your outdoor space is filled with trees and large shrubs, you are inviting squirrels and other climbing animals, including raccoons and opossums. But you can learn to live with and deal with these animals. Or in some cases, the animals can be made to feel less welcome using other methods discussed for each animal (see Chapter 6).

Strategic planting of plants desirable to animals you consider pests is important. Where you plant that hosta bed may mean the difference between enjoying your hosta collection or deciding which salad dressing to serve the deer as they eat at the hosta buffet. Plant those special plants closer to your home: in pots on the deck, outside the front or back door, in the fenced-in backyard or out front where the deer never go. Take a few minutes to look around your neighborhood. Some of your neighbors' outdoor spaces thrive despite the pressure of the pests causing havoc in your garden. Get to know those gardeners. Ask what is working for them. Sometimes, making your yard more lush and healthy makes it less desirable to the pests. Those pests head to other spaces they prefer more.

If you don't feel comfortable talking to your successful neighbor gardeners, be observant and copy what seems to work for them. Where have they put their fruit trees so deer don't eat them all winter? Do they strategically fence in those tender, delicious plants, but, because the plants look so good, you don't even notice the fencing? Have they hidden those plant gems amongst ornamental grasses and fragrant herbs? Do they plant mostly daffodils and forego tulips that only seem to tempt deer, rabbits, and squirrels?

RETHINK YOUR LAWN

If you love your turf (and lots of people do), there are things you can do to minimize pest damage. Perhaps you thought I would say pull out all the turf and plant native plants and trees? If you have children or pets, you may need space for them to romp. A nice turf can highlight a beautiful garden. Turf can cool your yard and soften the sound of the neighborhood. Now, here comes the crazy idea—consider adding white clover to your turf.

We Americans have had a love affair with our turf for a long time. Before the 1950s, we allowed clover and dandelions in the grass. Mostly because we

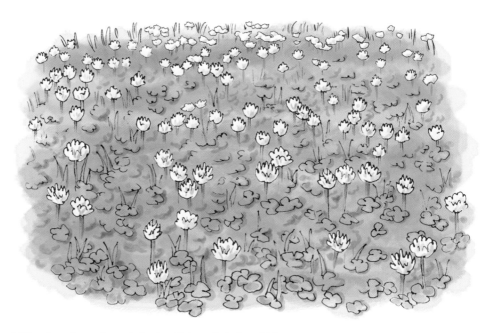

Adding clover to your lawn distracts rabbits and similar nibbling pests from lilies and other vulnerable plants.

didn't have all the herbicides we do now. But in the 1950s, herbicides became popular. The seed and chemical companies were pretty smart. If you kill all the broadleaf weeds—that may actually benefit the grass—you now have to fertilize the grass. If you cut the grass shorter you may need to water more and use more fertilizer and herbicides. Instead of a short manageable meadow we were to aspire to billiard table-flat green lawns.

If you add clover to your lawn, you may find the rabbits prefer it (and truly they do) rather than your lilies. Woodchucks too prefer clover—it is one of their favorites. Clover is also a great bee attractor and often found in "bee lawns." Bee lawns are an alternative to traditional grassy spaces that include low-growing plants that flower and provide nectar and pollen for the pollinators. This may include creeping thyme, clover, low-growing sedums, violets, or Canadian ginger. Fescue is also the grass often used in these mixes, as it is a slower-growing grass and doesn't need the fertilizers that Kentucky bluegrass does. Some of these plants can take a bit of foot traffic and others very little, so they need to be planned and planted according to how the area is to be used. You may find that as you increase the diversity in your landscape, your pest problems seem to lessen or even disappear entirely.

Clover is also a nitrogen fixer. The nodules on its roots allow the plant to pull nitrogen from the air and store it in those nodules. As the roots die, the nodules release that nitrogen back into the soil to the grass roots. If you use a 30-0-15 fertilizer on your lawn, that first number represents nitrogen, the very thing that clover provides free.

The clover will not need to be mowed as often as your grass may need to be mowed. More time saved for you. As you add diversity to your turf grass you may notice it seems healthier. It is more able to grow thick and lush. More able to withstand some insect damage, or avoid damage altogether, because the soil is so healthy that none of the "bad" soil insects get out of control. Using products on your lawn that aren't organic or natural may decrease the soil health and resilience of your lawn, forcing you to use even more products.

What about those dandelions? If you can, let them be! Just mow the flowers before they go to seed—it will keep your neighbors happier. The dandelions are an early flowering plant. They may be one of the few plants in flower when female bumblebees come out of hibernation and are starving. Just recently, the rusty patched bumblebee was put on the endangered list. Yes, a bumblebee is endangered. There may even be some already extinct, as they have not been seen in years. To me, the bumblebee is an iconic part of summer—hearing the lazy buzz and seeing that seemingly impossible-to-fly bee slowly fly past is a treat I enjoy every time.

Dandelions have a big, hardy, deep taproot that breaks up the compact soil and draws nutrients from far underground. As it is mowed and the leaves left on the lawn to decompose, those nutrients are available again for the grass. Even dandelions feed the turf grass for you, while they loosen the soil and allow channels to be created so rain can be kept there and filtered back to the aquifers below rather than run off into our lakes and streams.

How can a nice lawn filled with clover help control pests? Remember, rabbits and woodchucks prefer the clover, so they may leave your plants and vegetable garden alone. Also, while the rabbits enjoy clover snacks, the hawks

Loose birdseed and unsecured trash bins are magnets for squirrels, raccoons, and other pests.

or owls on their perches high above are preparing to grab a rabbit or two to feed their own young.

A healthy, diverse outdoor space may entice some pests to areas where they do less damage. This outdoor space may be uncomfortable for many animal pests because you are outside in it more often because it is a wonderfully beautiful and energizing space to be in. Your healthy outdoor space may create barriers that some pests don't want to cross (thick hedges) or too much cover—it could hide predators—or offer no space for pests to hang out. It may be so diverse that no one thing is in abundance enough to attract a pest—or if you do have lots of say, hostas, they are spread everywhere or tucked safely near your home, out of the reach of pests that love to nibble them.

Because your outdoor space is so full of bird life, the insects are kept in check. The birds have so much other food they don't bother your crops. Doesn't it sound like a paradise? And it can be your paradise if you wish.

KEEP THINGS TIDY

The final aspect of a healthy garden can be simple cleanup and neatness.

Store woodpiles far away from your home so mice and, perhaps, snakes will be far from your foundation. (If you build it, they will come.)

Compost bins and piles are great for creating your own compost, but if you put the wrong things in the pile, like meat or cheese or bones, you are inviting pests into your yard. Keep the compost piles clean and place them away from your home slightly—not so far; you want easy to access to them. Some locations may require you keep them covered. If this is the case in your town, watch to make sure they stay damp enough—when water is needed pull off the cover before a rainstorm.

Spilled birdseed will attract ground-feeding birds, but it will also attract mice and other pests. Clean up the spilled seed or feed only what the birds (and squirrels) will eat in one day.

SELECTING EFFECTIVE PRODUCTS AND METHODS FOR PEST CONTROL

3

You have planted your garden to the best of your ability. It looks pretty good—or it will when it grows. The lawn is coming in nicely and promises to be a great place for the children to play and the adults to enjoy the sunshine.

The patio is beautiful, benches and tables complemented by plants, all luring you to dine al fresco or enjoy a morning cup of coffee or afternoon cocktail.

Time passes, things seem to go well, then suddenly, not so well. The raccoons and skunks have found the lawn and are digging it up. The deer are eating the hostas you so carefully planted. The aphids have invaded the *Rudbeckia* and Japanese beetles cover the grapes and roses. Squirrels are destroying your just-planted containers; spittlebugs are found on nearly all your plants; rabbits have eaten the lilies to the ground and the herons have taken your prized koi from the pond. Your idyllic yard and garden are turning into a battleground—and you are prepping for battle.

Living in the city helps in some respects. In larger urban areas, the deer will not be much of a problem, but the squirrels, chipmunks, and rabbits are. If you live near a nature area or a wild area, or even a golf course, you may experience more animal pest issues. I bring this up because so many people move to those locations for the beauty of nature and then object when they must deal with more of it than anticipated. But you don't need to live near a nature center to encounter pests—as more and more of us add diversity to our landscapes, and our cities manage the wild areas more organically, we will find that the number of animals we may see will increase. Rabbits and other small animals find and fill new niches that we create, adapting to the changes we make to lessen the hardscape and bring in nature to our homes. While that may seem to suggest we pave over more wild areas to prevent pests, actually the reverse is true. As we can diversify our habitat, the pest problems often actually lessen. Nature reaches balances more easily when one thing is not overwhelming every other feature. Sometimes it is difficult to await this balance, and we can mitigate damage to our landscape by our action.

FENCING

In many cases, you can simply change the movement of pests by strategic fencing—either by fencing them out or by using fencing in such a way to divert them to less problematic areas. This may be your best option, although it can be expensive and, perhaps, not the most beautiful option. None of us wants to live in a fenced-in compound, but we do want our yards protected.

Recently I put in a chain-link fence around my yard. Not to stop the deer (not a problem for my area), but to limit some human incursions into my gardens and to keep my chickens fenced in when they are allowed into certain areas. This fence did keep out most of the rabbits, but one did find its way in during winter and, because it was safe from most other predators, proceeded to dine happily on apple tree branches and even appears to have girdled one of the fruit tree—eaten the bark all the way around the base of the tree. Trees move nutrients and water up and down the full length of the truck from the leaves to the roots, an activity that happens just under the bark in the living layer of the tree, so if this is destroyed, there is no way for the nutrients and water to move from one area of the tree to the other. I had not protected those trees with their usual winter fencing because I thought they were safe. Apparently, my fence has some spots I

need to look at more closely. Most people hate the thought of a chain-link fence—they don't like the look and I understand that. I see my fence as a trellis. I plan to grow many vines and vegetables on the fencing to soften the look. I put a "chain-link trellis" around my yard.

Wooden fences work well to keep out some animals. Deer may not jump a wooden fence, as they can't see what is on the other side. Squirrels will see your wooden fence simply as another squirrel highway to enjoy in the neighborhood. Depending on the style of the wood fence, rabbits and armadillos may or may not be able to wiggle through it; woodchucks won't climb it, although they may dig under it if they know there is a good food source on the other side. Solid wood fences will impact the wind your garden experiences; you may find that your garden is windier in some areas and much calmer in others. This can influence the health of your plants and what insects you see in your landscapes,

Wooden fences are a good option for deer—if they can't see what's on the other side, they're less likely to try to jump over.

which is something to consider when choosing a style of fencing. Many cities and towns have laws and restrictions on fencing. Investigate these requirements for your community. If the laws and regulations need revamping, get like-minded people together to talk to your city lawmakers and get the requirements changed. If you live in a planned or gated community, it may be harder to get the laws changed as people moved to that community to live as it was presented to them at the time. Unless many of your fellow community members are experiencing the same pest issues and care about the situation as much as you do, it may be more than you can do to change fencing laws to protect your yard and garden. If that is the case, you may need plan B.

There are other ways to protect your yard and garden. You can fence in specific parts of your garden or even specific plants, either temporarily or permanently. When planting new trees, if deer, rabbits, voles, or mice could be an issue, consider protecting each tree with a cylinder of hardware cloth. You can purchase a 3×25-foot roll at the local hardware store or your big box store for about $30 per roll. This will protect many plants. I like to use hardware cloth rather than chicken wire because hardware cloth deters the voles and mice; they can't get through the ¼-inch holes. Cut sections of hardware cloth, or screen, about 16 to 24 inches long. Create a cylinder that is about 5 to 10 inches in diameter. Place this around the tree after you plant it correctly and water it in. Then apply the mulch to the surrounding area outside the cylinder as far as you wish. This cylinder will prevent animals from gnawing on the tasty tender bark, especially in winter. It will also keep lawn mowers and Weedwackers from damaging the tree's trunk and bark. (People may damage tree trunks nearly as much as animals do!) The cylinder also keeps the mulch away from the trunk—never mulch up to

Wrapping hardware cloth around the trunk of a tree protects it from girdling—especially a concern for young, tender trees or during the winter when rabbits and mice have fewer other options.

Rabbit fencing is very effective, but it won't deter squirrels or racoons—and determined baby bunnies are small enough to squeeze through the holes in some netting.

the truck or stem of any plant. You can leave this cylinder on the tree until it is big enough that it nearly touches the cylinder or it acquires the thick rough bark that will protect it. If you live in an area that gets snow, you may need to add height extensions to keep deer and rabbits away. Deer can reach up to 6 or 8 feet and rabbits can stand up about 1 foot higher than snow level. During winter, you may want to add protection up to the first branch of your tree if deer are an issue. Use this cylinder instead of the white plastic corrugated cylinders that often come with new trees. If your tree comes with this plastic protection, cut it, rather than pull it, off the trunk to avoid scratching and damaging the bark. Once you put on the hardware cloth cylinder, your eyes will start to ignore it quickly and soon you will not even notice it, but you will notice your tree stays safe.

You can also fence off your gardens with decorative fencing, chicken wire, or rabbit fencing. These fences will keep rabbits and skunks out of your garden, but they will not slow squirrels or raccoons. There are ways to use fencing

A flexible fence supported by a section that lays on the ground is effective if you're fighting climbing critters. It stays upright but isn't steady enough for them to scale. Fencing on the ground will also keep out digging pests, such as rabbits and raccoons. This may be easier than burying the fence several feet underground.

to deter or slow some climbing pests, such as raccoons or opossums, or even armadillos. Use a fence that can be installed so 6 to 12 inches lays on the ground outside the garden. The rest of the fence, then, stands upright but not steady. Leaving the fence on the ground prevents digging under the fence to get into the garden. The unsteadiness of the fence deters climbing over it. Install your fence *before* you plant the garden. Once the fence is up, most pests will ignore the goodies inside because they don't know they're there. It is only when the rabbit or raccoon knows there is a meal to be had that they do almost anything to get over, under, or around the fence. This is good to remember in autumn too. Install your temporary fencing in fall and you won't have to worry that the rabbits will eat your newly emerging tender plants in spring. Trust me, the plants come up before you realize they are there and the garden pests are watching and waiting. They know when things are growing or nearly ripe in our gardens before we do. Their very lives depend on this.

REPELLENTS

Make a visit to your local nursery or garden center. I tend to rely on these a bit more because they are locally owned and I can support my local businesses. The owners have a bigger stake in keeping me as a customer and, often, are

You'll find a wide array of repellent options you can try in your garden. Be sure to tailor your choice to the pests you're targeting and the plants to which you're applying them.

more knowledgeable about local pest problems and what works the best. The pest control aisle in most garden/nursery stores is filled with various chemical control methods—some are repellents, some are poisons. There may even be some interesting products that claim protection or prevention.

If you do decide to use a human-made chemical, please follow the directions. This is something I can't say strongly enough, so, forgive me if I repeat myself. *Read*, *understand*, and *follow* all the instructions of *every* product you use in your yard or garden. Read the entire label—yes, the whole thing. Know what you are getting into or what could be getting into you. More is not better. Don't double the strength or use the product for an off-label use. The label is the *law*. Think it through. This is your garden's health and very survival we are talking about here. It is important. Timing of sprays is important.

- Don't spray products on plants during the heat of the day or they burn.
- Decide if the pest is still present before you spray. Sometimes, by the time we see the damage, the pest has moved on.
- If you are dealing with a hungry rabbit or deer, prevention is best. Spray before you see the damage.
- Use different kinds of repellents as pests become used to one kind. Rotate the garlic spray with the mint and then another "fragrance" before you go back to the garlic.

Repellents can be one of your most effective responses to pest problems. Wild animals and insects have highly evolved senses when it comes to smells or fragrances. That said, remember they live in our human world filled with pollution,

Pesticides may solve your pest problem, but they can also damage your plants. Avoid applying in the heat of the day, and always read the directions and warnings on store-bought products.

car exhaust, man-made plastics, perfumes, and, just to be honest, stinky humans. The repellents you can use in your yard and gardens usually cost between $10 and $20. Remember to use them as the label suggests.

Repellents act in a few different ways. One is to be so obnoxious to the pest that it avoids the area. It may be a strong smell, like rotten eggs or garlic, or even a smell that proclaims "danger," like blood meal (dried blood from slaughterhouses) or a predator urine.

Blood Meal

Blood meal works because the animals smell the blood. They believe that something has died there. Because most of our pests are prey animals, they need to be aware of their surroundings. If an animal has "died" there and the blood smell is still evident, perhaps the predator is still around and it is not a safe place to be. Blood meal can be purchased in dried form, usually in 3- to 5-pound bags for $10 to $20 per bag. Use gloves when sprinkling it in the area you wish to protect, such as the outside of a garden to thwart rabbits

Fox urine will scare away rabbits and squirrels, but it won't work on deer.

or chipmunks from entering. It should be safe to use in most gardens. Blood meal contains a small amount of nitrogen and so will feed your soil and can be used as an organic source of nitrogen for organic gardeners. You may not want to use blood meal if you own a dog, or are planning on using it in an area open to the public, as it can attract dogs to the area. Blood meal will also be washed into the soil by rain, watering, or even a heavy dew, so you need to reapply it often depending on the weather or how you water your garden.

Predator Urine

Predator urine is another repellent option. You may want to investigate the collection method used to get this urine to see how humane it is in your eyes.

If you decide to use it, use the correct urine. Fox urine will not frighten deer—they are not in a predator/prey relationship—but coyote or wolf urine will. Fox or coyote urine will work for rabbits and squirrels too.

When using the urine, position it in your yard where the predator normally would—usually about 2 feet or lower in the yard, and often against a tree or rock or even a pile of soil.

These urine repellents may work for a time but, eventually, the squirrels or rabbits or deer realize there is no true threat and ignore it. Change it up with some other repellent when this happens. During cold or especially rainy weather, the product may need to be reapplied more often.

Fragrance Repellents

Other repellents are herbal or fragrance based. I have found these to be quite successful. Strong smells, such as oranges or citrus, may repel cats. Mint, clove, or other spices or herbs work well for mice and rabbits and other small animals. Because prey animals use their sense of smell to find their food and keep safe, these strongly fragranced repellents can overwhelm their sensitive senses or disguise the food they are looking for. These repellents are also priced about $10 to $20 per bottle or container. Some are liquid and sprayed on the plants or area to protect, others are powders sprinkled on the soil, and some are scent-infused substances that can be placed around the areas to be protected. The latter are often sold in little bags that can be placed in your grill, or stored in a boat or car over winter to protect against mice nesting there.

Orange, mint, and clove are strong scents that deter pests without being unpleasant to humans.

This type of repellent should be used according to label instructions. Some are okay to use on food crops; others are not. All need to be re-applied as directed. Hot weather and precipitation can shorten the time they remain effective. Even winter's cold may affect the fragrance—it does not travel as far in cold weather, so pests may get closer to the food source than you want them to, and the cold may shorten the length of effectiveness.

Make Your Own Repellents

Essential oils are easily available by mail or from your local pharmacy, grocery, or other store. These essential oils are concentrated and should be treated with respect as you use them. These essential oils are not perfume oils; they will be labeled essential oil. Never apply them to your skin or ingest them. This means don't spray them on food plants either. However, you can spray the soil surface or fencing around your garden to repel some pests you encounter. You need a carrier oil or sticker agent to keep the essential oil in place. Carrier oils and sticker agents are things that extend the essential oil and help them to stick and stay where you spray them. You can use olive or vegetable oil as a carrier/sticker agent. The soap is added as an additional repellent and it helps the product to stay where it is placed also. Never use dish detergent. These are degreasers and may strip the plant leaves of their healthy surface oils. These may only last a week or so in your garden and you will need to apply them again.

1. Fill a 16- or 32-ounce spray bottle three-fourths full of water.
2. Add 10 to 20 drops of peppermint essential oil (scaling up or down depending on how much water you're using).
3. Add 1 teaspoon dish soap*, such as Ivory. Both fragranced or nonfragranced varieties work.
4. Add 1 teaspoon vegetable, canola, or olive oil (this is your carrier oil). Use the cheapest oil you have available. Don't waste your good olive oil on this.
5. Cover the bottle and shake well. Spray this solution on clean surfaces where you have seen ants in your home or on the patio. Spray it around the foundation of your home or stairs to repel mice or ants from entering. Reapply as needed. Do not apply this directly on plants, people, or pets.

* Use soap rather than detergent, as detergent will strip oils from plants. Even though you are not using this on plants, it is easiest to only use soap in your homemade preparations just in case there is some overspray.

In winter or during a drought, all bets are off with these repellents. And even in good times, if the pest population has increased too much, there may be too much pressure to find food that animals ignore any repellents you use. The will to live is strong.

As mentioned, these pests live among humans and so are used to many smells. They soon learn that new smells may be a warning, or something to ignore. This means we humans have to be willing to change it up occasionally. If one repellent seems to work for a while and then does not, change to a different repellent.

You can also use herbal tea as a repellent. I have used this successfully, when planting tulip bulbs or flower containers, to deter squirrels from digging up my planting efforts.

Plant as usual. Brew a strong pot of tea—peppermint, orange, cinnamon, rosemary, or oregano. Let the tea cool to room temperature. Remove the teabags, if you use them. Water the newly planted tulip bulbs in well and top off the watering with a drench of the fragrant tea. You can even tear apart the tea bags and sprinkle the used leaves over the soil. Also water newly planted containers with this fragrant tea. Any strong-smelling herb or spice will work. Experiment with what you have in the cupboard and remember to change it up. One day use peppermint, the next planting day use cinnamon. This works to disguise the scent of freshly dug soil in the squirrel's territory. Squirrels are territorial and want to know what was dug up or buried in "their" territory.

Herbal tea disguises the smell of freshly dug earth, which will call squirrels like a beacon.

Synthetic Chemical Repellents

To repel deer, there are some great chemical or man-made repellents. I suggest changing them up every month or so. If you plan to use them to protect food plants or fruit trees, make sure the repellent is labeled safe for food. I will repeat this often—it is very important.

Some people hang bars of soap in the garden to repel the deer and rabbits. Irish Spring is a favorite, but any strong-smelling soap will work. One thing about this: Soap is washed away by the rain or watering and gets into the soil. There are many beneficial insects in the soil that may be killed by the soap. Soap is a poison. So, perhaps, hang it where the resulting current of liquid soap flows into a nongarden space, such as the lawn or a mulched area.

Mechanical Deterrents

As mentioned, there are many devices on the market that are supposed to prevent or repel pests. The ultrasonic devices don't work that well. Animals adjust quickly to noises we humans produce and soon learn to ignore many of the scare tactics. One device that does seem to work well is the motion-activated sprinkler system. This is great to annoy and repel deer, raccoons, and even cats or nighttime human visitors to your yard.

Attach the sprinkler to your garden hose and turn on the water. When motion is sensed, the sprinkler goes off, which scares the animal, usually causing it to leave the area. Remember to turn off the water or the sensor if you are working in the garden or else you too will be sprayed. These usually cost about $100.

You can also hang noisy or flashy items in your yard. Aluminum pie plates flash and move in the wind and sun and may scare deer and birds away. Bits of white cotton, as from old T-shirts, can be hung at deer-tail height on a fence. When the wind blows, the white flashes and deer may mistake it for other deer tails flashing warnings. Hanging strings or plastic bottles, or even cans, on a walkway can deter deer as they wander through and bump into it—they don't like this and may change their route. Bird-scare tape, a shiny Mylar tape, can be hung from trees where it may flash and scare birds from your fruit trees.

Even simple plastic bags can be hung on sticks or a fence so they rustle with the breeze. Of course, they are not very attractive, so this may

A motion-activated sprinkler is a great way to startle and repel deer—and the occasional wandering human.

More Deterrent Sprays to Make at Home

Insecticidal Soap

This works best as a contact poison on soft-bodied insects. Mix and spray this early in the day on the insects you want to kill, when they are less active and easier to find. Test the spray on plants before you spray much of the plant. Some leaves may be burned. If this happens, don't use the spray on that plant again. Never spray plants in the sun, as burning may occur. Don't use on plants you want to eat.

Mix:

1 quart water
1 teaspoon dish soap, such as Ivory (not dish detergent or the soaps or detergents used in dishwashers)

Garlic/Rotten Egg Spray

The smell of this spray may deter a number of pests, including deer, rabbits, and many insects, such as caterpillars and beetles. The hot peppers may stop animals from nibbling on the plants. Spray it directly on plants and the soil around the garden to minimize damage. Don't use this on edible plants. Remember to test the spray on your plants first to make sure they are not damaged and never spray them while they are in direct sunlight.

You can purchase similar sprays if you don't want to mix your own. Some may be labeled for edible crops—use these if the pests are bothering your food crops.

In a blender:

1. Combine 3 or 4 raw eggs.
2. Add 1 to 2 cloves garlic, chopped.
3. Add 1 tablespoon Tabasco sauce.
4. Pour in 1 quart water.
5. Blend well and strain.

Sound is another way to scare off deer and other skittish pests. Wind chimes, or bottles and cans hung from string are deterents you can make yourself.

not be an option for many and they will start to break down quickly—so make sure they don't blow away and become litter.

Bottles hung from trees may "sing" as the wind blows over the tops. Empty them after it rains so you don't raise a new crop of mosquitoes in them.

You may find other items in the garden center. Plastic owls or snakes may scare the birds for a short time, but move them so they appear more lifelike. No owl sits in the same spot for ninety days at a time. I have even seen round balls with "eyes" drawn on them that are to scare away birds. I'm not sure how effective they are, but they could be an interesting talking point in your garden.

And, once again, chicken wire fence may help deter deer. Lay the fence in strips on the ground in the regular path the deer take through your yard. As the deer walk on it, the fencing will move and not be firm. The deer will not like this and they may change their route. You can pick up the fencing when you need to mow or the children want to play in that area.

All these items just make it uncomfortable and unpleasant for pests to remain in or keep coming to your yard.

TRAPPING

Another critter-control method is trapping. Please make sure this is legal in your area. Many animals are protected and, if protected, may not be trapped or killed, or may only be trapped by licensed professionals. If you hire a professional to trap your pest, make sure they are licensed, bonded, and knowledgeable about the task you require. Talk to your local nursery or garden center personnel as they may have good recommendations. If you are not comfortable with the person or company do not use them. At all times remember to keep yourself and your family and your wallet safe.

Once you have done your research and know you can legally trap the pest, purchase or rent the trap. Havahart traps are good no-kill traps. You need to know where you can release the pest once you have it trapped. Keep it in the trap for as short a time as possible, as being in the trap stresses the animal and you don't really want to hurt it. Release it where it will cause no more damage to your yard and garden and not damage anyone else's garden either.

Talk to your local extension agent or animal control office for the correct methods to remove the pests. Most animal control departments don't have the resources to remove the deer or raccoons, armadillos, skunks, opossums,

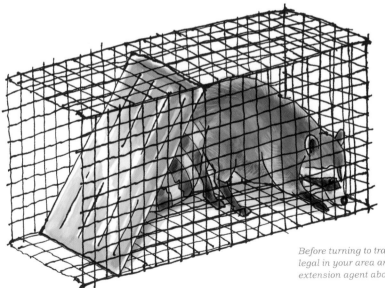

Before turning to trapping, be sure it's legal in your area and consult your local extension agent about best practices.

A Plea for Your Pets

I want to make a plea here—do not let your pets wander. Your dogs should be on leashes or in yards they can't escape from; your cats should not be allowed to roam the neighborhood, as they kill many of our songbirds. Cats allowed to roam have a much shorter lifespan than those kept inside. Our pets are not wild animals. They are companions bred to live with us. They must be treated with respect and care. If you can't do this, forego pet ownership.

or other mammals bothering your garden, but they may have ideas how to proceed in your area. These local agencies usually know which pests are causing the most damage and the legal ways to remove them. Avail yourself of these resources and follow their directions.

Many times, trapping a pest, such as a squirrel, is not the best way to proceed. Squirrels are territorial. Trying to relocate the trapped squirrel means you release it into an area where it will need to fight for new territory and fight to find food. In this instance, the most humane removal is to dispatch or kill the squirrel. Most of us don't have the heart to do this and, even if we do, the place vacated by the squirrel's removal will soon be filled by a new squirrel and our problems will continue. In this case it is better to "teach" the squirrels how to work in your garden with you.

If you have to dispatch or kill a pest, do so as humanely as possible and dispose of the carcass according to the laws in your city or county. Some harpoon killing traps are used for moles and voles. They are placed over the tunnels the animals use and, as the animal runs through the tunnel, the harpoon is triggered and stabs and kills (hopefully quickly) the animals. The traps are then removed and the animal carcass is left in the tunnel underground.

There are numerous ways to avoid killing but I know there may be instances where human safety may be involved. If you are dealing with a dangerous animal, such as a bear, cougar, or other large animal, animal control or your local department of natural resources will take care of the problem according to their procedures. If possible, once this is done, figure out how to avoid the problem again and make corrections in your yard or landscape. This may mean making sure to clean up any spilled birdseed that would have attracted the animal or making sure trash bins are secure. If dealing with big cats or even coyote problems, make sure to keep your pets inside during the evenings; don't let your cats roam free, and if small dogs need to go out at night, go with them. Some lighting of your landscape may be beneficial also. You don't have to light the entire yard—only strategic areas, such as decks, patios, or walkways. Adding some fencing will also work. Again, creating a diverse plant community will bring in a diverse animal population to your yard. If this population is diverse enough, there should be no single prey animal that will attract the attention of the predators. Harvest your garden and any fruits as they ripen so as not to leave overripened fruit to attract pests.

POISONS

Since this book concentrates on humane methods I mention the killers only in passing. There are poisons that work on many pest problems. Yes, you can set out poison bait if you think you have a mouse problem. The mice may take it and go off and die. However, the ramifications can be quite scary. That dead mouse may be eaten by your dog or cat and may poison or kill your pet. Pets and children can often get to the poison bait and may ingest it and die. Even if you keep your pets away, other wandering pets—or wild carrion animals, such as crows—may eat the dead mouse and some other family loses a pet

Not only are most poisons inhumane, but they can also have unintended consequences on animals beyond the ones you're targeting.

unnecessarily. Or perhaps the mouse is only slowed down by the poison, rather than killed—it may then be taken by a hawk or owl or eagle, the very birds we are hoping to help us with the rabbit population.

That dead mouse may also kill other animals—the raptor that feeds on it and the insects that clean up the carcass. So, by using a poison bait to kill one mouse, you may have killed many other creatures too.

Poisons may not be your best option. Remember nature abhors a vacuum. Once that mouse is dead, or even if you have successfully killed the entire mouse community, there is nothing to stop new mice from coming in. You have not solved the problem, just removed it temporarily. You need to change the environment.

WHEN TO CALL A PROFESSIONAL

Bringing in a professional to deal with your pest issue is always an option. In some cases—like dealing with fire ants or a huge beehive or an infestation of poisonous snakes or a hive of yellow jackets or carpenter ants living in your home—this may be your best option. This can be expensive. It may cost hundreds of dollars to remedy these infestations.

If you find a hive of bees on your property in a place where it is not safe for you or your family, have this hive removed. Rather than killing the bees, contact your local extension office or your state beekeepers' group. Often, there will be beekeepers available who will carefully remove the hive and relocate it to a safe place, frequently to the delight of a fellow beekeeper. Our pollinators need our protection and we should do what we can to prevent their numbers from decreasing.

Though poisons should not be an option for removing honeybees or beehives if at all possible, some people are allergic to bee stings, so it is important to protect humans as well. In this case, the safety of humans is more important than allowing the beehive to remain.

Your extension office can direct you to local pest control agencies or offer guidelines on what to look for in a pest control/removal company. It will probably not give specific company recommendations as it is not allowed to favor one business over another, but the lists of questions and other ideas to consider are helpful. If you live in an area where fire ants or poisonous snakes are issues, the local pest removal companies can deal with these pests. These insects and snakes are dangerous—be careful and let the professionals handle it. Again, it may be a few hundred to a few thousand dollars to remedy the problem. Talk to neighbors, check with the local business community for recommendations—do your investigation so you get what you pay for and hire a reputable company.

Should you find carpenter ants in your home, again, a professional may be the best option to find and remove the nest and, if needed, a construction company may have to repair the structural damage. This will cost hundreds or, yes, even thousands of dollars if the infestation is large or the damage is significant. As in most cases, you can minimize the damage to your property and wallet if you catch the problem early.

ATTRACTING BEFICIAL INSECTS AND ANIMALS

ATTRACTING BENEFICIAL INSECTS AND ANIMALS

4

I expect my plants to do most if not all the work for me. I expect all my plants to fulfill two or three functions, or even more. That is called stacking functions in the view of permaculture. In my yard, I grow a smaller viburnum, 'Blue Muffin'. This plant is to be a foundation plant, provide nectar to pollinators as it blooms and food for birds with its ripe berries. For years this plant was infested by aphids. The stress was so great that the flowers would abort and no fruit would be growing. I never let the aphid population reach a critical level to attract predator insects like ladybugs. One year I decided to just wait. Sure enough, when I allowed the aphids to reach that population, the ladybugs came, laid eggs, and the adults and larvae ate the aphids. This would not have happened if I had killed the aphid population. But now I have a ladybug population in my garden and they can move from plant to plant and eat aphids as the aphids appear.

By not interfering or even adding anything as simple as insecticidal soap, we can set up our landscapes to be more self sufficient. We need to build safe places for our predators to grow and multiply so that they can take care of pests for us.

We can make our gardens very attractive to beneficial bugs by doing just a few easy things.

Plant pollinator-friendly flowers, such as coneflowers, to welcome bees, butterflies, and other beneficial insects to your garden.

AVOID PESTICIDES

Don't use pesticides at all if you can. If you must use a pesticide, use it early in the morning before pollinators are flying and many bugs are moving. That way you have a better chance of targeting the desired insect and less chance of hurting the innocent or desired bugs. Again, I remind you to read, understand, and follow all label instructions on any pesticide you use.

There are many alternatives to consider before resorting to petroleum-based chemicals. Repellents that use fragrance (see pages 53 to 55) may work to disguise a targeted plant from a pest, or you could use a barrier to bar access. Hot pepper or bad-tasting "repellents" may work for many insects—one bite and they are away. Water sprayed on pests can remove them. Insecticidal soaps, while still chemicals, may be less impactful on your outdoor spaces. Handpicking is always an option—if the insects are large enough. So often, if we see the problem early or even anticipate it, we can avoid using pesticides—and we keep our outdoor spaces safer and save money too.

LET THE PESTS ATTRACT THE PREDATORS

Another way we can attract those beneficial bugs to our yards is to let the bad bug populations increase enough to entice the good bugs to set up residence in our garden. It may be hard to watch the bad bug population grow and just hope the goods bugs show up. But, if you never allow the bad bug population to grow, the good bugs will not show up or stay. Think of it like this: If a ladybug is looking to lay her eggs, which area will she choose? A desert of a place with no food or a garden filled with possibilities of fat aphids and other soft-bodied insects? She will, of course, choose the garden filled with insects for her young to eat.

Usually, if you have a healthy garden environment, allowing the pests to reach that critical level is all you need to do—the predators will come. If, however, your garden is a sterile environment or a monoculture of only one plant (or very few), you may find that this is not the case. There is no place for them, only a place for their food—your pest. To address this, you can take the place of the predator and remove the pest, or you can begin to make your yard more diverse and healthy. It will take time and effort, but you will build a healthy outdoor space where nature will do the harder work and you can have more fun.

CREATE INSECT HOMES

Other things beneficial to our gardens are places for the young to grow. Garden debris creates wonderful homes for insects to live in. Consider leaving some small piles of leaves, stones, or twigs around the garden. You can create an insect hotel that can be a wonderful garden sculpture or a hidden feature in the back of your garden. This could consist of a mix of twigs and logs in various sizes with piles of leaves and twigs in various rooms. Design a structure of bricks and boards and fill each niche with different-sized logs and twigs. Bore holes into some of the logs to entice a variety of insects.

In addition, insects are cold-blooded creatures. Place some rocks in areas where they will catch the early sun for insects to sit on and warm up. If you install any Mason bee houses or other insect homes, place them where they are warmed early in the morning and protected from harsh winter winds. If precipitation is heavy in your area make sure the insect homes have some protection from the rains. This same advice applies if you install bat houses. Beekeepers use a similar placement for their beehives.

Those rock piles may also attract some cold-blooded animals that will help in your pest control. Snakes, toads, and lizards all are wonderful insect predators. I understand many people are uncomfortable around these animals, but just make some noise as you head into their part of the yard and they should hide from you. The warm rocks will help them to thaw out on those chilly mornings, and the rocks could be places they want to live or hibernate over winter.

Mulch in the garden is also a great place for insects to hide or live. The mulch allows the soil to hold on to the moisture received and helps mitigate the

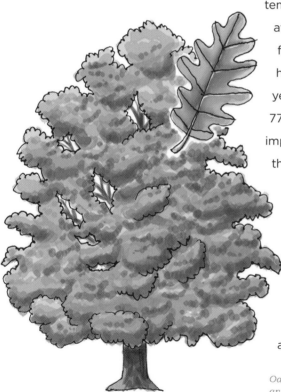

temperature swings from the sun, keeping plant roots at a more even temperature. Most plants benefit from this. You will find that mulch will become home to many kinds of beetles, centipedes, and, yes, even slugs (more on the slugs later, see page 77). The beetles, centipedes, and earwigs are all important in any healthy ecosystem. They help eat the dead insects (or animals) and break down organic matter so it can continue composting. They may be creepy and a little scary but, before you instinctively kill them, I suggest you research what you have and what that insect does.

Before you cover all the soil with mulch, consider leaving some areas mulch free. This is where many native ground bees live. Leave the areas directly under a shrub bare—no mulch should

Oak trees can support hundreds of species of caterpillars and butterflies and provide a home for birds.

ever touch the stem or trunks of trees, shrubs, or plants anyway. Leaving this area bare means it's protected from the rains and a bit drier. This is exactly the place a ground bee may enjoy living. They are gentle, solitary creatures who pollinate lots of our native plants and many of our food crops. By leaving this area free for them you may see an increase in your flower or food production.

If you can only plant one tree in your yard, consider an oak. It will support more than five hundred species of caterpillars and butterflies—not to mention all the other insects and birds found there. Every plant and tree should contribute to your landscape in some fashion. If an oak is not for you, perhaps oak wilt is endemic in your area or the soil pH is not conducive to an oak, research which native trees grew there before the area was built up. There are state land-use maps that will help with this, or contact a local native plant group or your extension office.

If we increase the number of native plants we grow, we will increase the number of, and the health of, our native insect species. Be prepared to see some insects feeding on these plants. That is one of their functions in the environment you are creating—to be a food source or habitat for the insects you want in your landscape. In my yard, when I see weeds being eaten, I know the plants I am growing for my food are not being eaten—usually, at least, this is how it works.

You can also create housing for birds in your yard. Birds nest at certain heights and in a variety of shrubs and trees, so if your yard contains a variety of plants—some shorter and some taller—you may find more birds nesting. Of course, you can also supply the correctly placed bird houses.

If your landscape has a dead tree that can safely be left standing, please do so for the sake of raptors. These snags will allow the hawks and eagles to perch as they search for prey. The owls will use them at night. Many of our native birds and pollinators nest in cavities in trees. Large trees may support nests of larger

Tall trees and dead trees (or "snags"), if they are safe, make great places for raptors to survey the area for food—many of the animals they prey on are the ones you would like to keep out of your yard.

birds or at least places for them to perch and search for food. Do what you can to increase the plant diversity in your landscape. By keeping many shrubs, you also allow the songbirds protection from birds of prey.

PROVIDE FOOD AND WATER

Insects need water so keep the birdbaths filled. Add floating sticks or twigs so insects, such as bees, can land and get a drink of water without falling in and drowning. Add some moist sand for butterflies to puddle (drink moisture from the moist sand and draw out minerals they need from it). If the water feature on your property is a pond or waterfall, create a very shallow space where plants or sticks are available for insects to land on while they get a drink of water. Of course, make sure all the water is either moving, stocked with fish to eat mosquito larvae, or that you change still containers every two days and refill them with fresh water. Removing standing water also prevents mosquito larvae—the wrigglers—from hatching or attaining adulthood. Keeping water available at all times in your landscape for wildlife will attract many birds, who will eat the bad (and, yes, some good) bugs; other animals such as raptors or owls will enjoy a fresh drink of water, as will frogs or lizards that inhabit your home, and pollinators such as butterflies and bees. This will add dimension to your landscape, and may also head

A water source is important for the beneficial animals and insects you want in your yard.

off a common squirrel problem: that of them eating your tomatoes, which is usually motivated by the squirrels being thirsty (see pages 19 and 102).

Consider adding a rain garden to your landscape if it works for you. These gardens are meant to function as brief water-holding areas where the first ½ inch of rain or so can be held to sink into the soil and renew the aquifer, which cleans the water before it enters our watersheds and renews our groundwater sources. These rain gardens only hold water for twenty-four hours, but during that time they will attract animals to drink and bathe. The plants they grow add more diversity to our landscapes and provide food and building materials for our birds and insects.

Milkweed is an excellent food source for Monarch butterflies, which both add beauty and pollinate your garden.

Water is your friend in your landscape. Use the water you dump from the containers to water nearby plants. Design your landscape plantings so water-hungry plants are near your water sources. It helps to keep everything more sustainable.

If you want to attract butterflies, provide a food source for their young and plants that provide nectar for the adults. To attract monarch butterflies, grow milkweed for the young and nectar-filled plants such as asters, coneflowers, or liatris for the adult butterflies. This works for all insects—provide the plants or insects they need to feed their young or themselves. All stages of the insect's life should be provided for. Some of these plants may be more aggressive than you prefer, or not as attractive as you may want. In these cases, place these plants on the outer edges of your landscape or leave a place in your landscape that you seldom visit or maintain—all within the laws of your town or city.

This unmanicured area will soon feature interesting flowers and plants that you never planned for. And soon there will be wildlife, birds, bees, and other insects that find a home there and flourish. This richness will spill over into the maintained area of your landscape and bring a new dimension to the healthy ecoscape you are creating. When you must weed, do so carefully and refrain from using any poisons. Because the plants will be varied, it is unlikely you will see a large infestation of any one insect in this area.

THINK ABOUT WIND

Another impact we seldom consider is wind. A light breeze for us can be a hurricane for insects. Create some areas in your yard where the wind is slowed. You can do this with partial fencing. A full wooden fence with no holes or places for wind to blow through actually speeds the wind and creates updrafts and downdrafts—the very thing you are trying to avoid. Instead, install a fence with spaces between the boards or plant a variety of shrubs and trees as they too slow or reroute the breezes in your yard. You may find you enjoy this as well as you can sit on your deck or patio without being blown away. If you live in a colder climate, strategically place these structures or shrubs and trees so they break or slow the cold northwest winds that can desiccate or even kill plants. Even without leaves, the branches and twigs will work for this effort. Consider adding a trellis, which will break the wind and slow it down even without a vine on it; a trellis with a flowering vine that attracts your favorite bird or butterfly may be even better.

If your area is subject to intense sun or heat, a shade cloth will ease the stress of the plants, and birds and insects may enjoy a break from the direct sun as well. This cloth can still let in the rain but will just add a bit of protection from the overhead sun. It may even be placed over where you sit and enjoy your garden to allow you to be out in your garden at times that you may have avoided it in the past.

BE AWARE OF INSECT BEHAVIOR

I used to have a terrible fear of bees and wasps. I had never been stung; it was simply fear. Then I began to study them. Bees are very beneficial, as we all know, for pollinating our plants. One-third of our food is the direct result of this pollination! They are gentle creatures that only react when threatened. I am an adult human—they are tiny insects—so why should I fear them? Even after being stung by a yellow jacket—hiding in a bag I picked up—the pain was not as bad as I feared, but it was still painful; I knew wasps were much more aggressive.

Again, some research was needed. Bees and wasps are more aggressive in late summer as they frantically forage for protein. During the rest of the spring and summer they are not as aggressive, partly due to the food and nectar

Honey bee—they are usually "fuzzy" or hairy

Hornet—has a wider head and rounder body

Yellow jacket wasp— slightly hairy

Hornet—usually smooth-bodied

Bees, wasps, and similar insects may seem scary, but they generally won't harm humans if left to their own devices. They also can benefit your garden by pollinating flowers and preying on plant-damaging pests. Be sure you know which one you're dealing with.

freely available during those times and the fact that the hives are being built and populations may be smaller. Then, one day, I found a dead caterpillar on the sidewalk. The yellow jackets were buzzing around. By the next day they had cleaned up most of the dead insect—aha!—another reason to let yellow jackets just be when I could. They are a part of nature's great cleanup crew, helping recycle all those dead insects and birds. Now I simply ignore them and they seem to ignore me. In fact, I may even be heard to tell them quietly, "There is nothing here for you," if they are buzzing around a project I am working on— painting, planting, weeding, etc. So far, our truce seems to be holding. I don't bother them and they don't bother me. This is not to say you must allow them to build a nest right over your doorway or near where your children or pets play. There is a place for everything and you are entitled to keep yourself and children safe. Even those insects we may label as "bad" at first may really be the good guys. We just need to understand them better.

If someone in the family is allergic to bee stings or has pollen allergies, there are still many flowers you can plant to attract those good bugs and pollinators to your yard. Plant them downwind and far from where the allergic person will be. Many

Strategically planted shrubs reduce the impact of wind, which is good for both insects and plants.

insect-pollinated flowers have pollen that is too heavy to be windblown, and unless the allergic person is sniffing the flowers, she may not be bothered by the allergy.

There are some insects we really don't want to see in our landscapes at all, a prime example being mosquitoes. To minimize mosquito activity in your yard, make sure to empty any standing water every three days and replace it with fresh water. If you have rain barrels, make sure they are covered so mosquitoes cannot access the water to lay their eggs. Get rid of any incidental standing water that you find on your property. If your climate is humid and mosquitoes are a major problem, you may need to wear repellants or enjoy your garden during the daylight hours when most mosquitoes are not out as much. If you are entertaining outdoors during prime mosquito hours, you may want to burn citronella torches or incense sticks sold for the purpose of repelling mosquitoes. Birds and dragonflies are among the predators of mosquitoes, so making these predators welcome in your yard goes a long way to minimizing the populations. If there are mosquito-related health issues in your area, be sure to follow the guidelines suggested by your local health department.

During the fall, many insects may try to move inside with us to escape the colder weather—Asian lady beetles and box elder bugs are among the most common offenders. Seal up any cracks or holes through which these insects may enter your home. You can also minimize their encroachment by clearing an area around the foundation of your house—a simple bare area of a foot or so between your home's foundation and the foundation plantings will minimize insects coming in. You can also apply repellents to this area to further deter would-be houseguests. If you are bringing inside any plants that spent the summer outside, make sure to wash the pots carefully and spray off any insects from the leaves. Keep these plants away from your other houseplants for three or four weeks to make sure no hitchhikers came in on them.

Ants getting in to the home can be minimized by removing what is attracting them: pet food, for example. These insects lay down scent trails to mark their way to and from their nests, so it is important to wipe any area you find ants with soap and water to destroy these trails. Mint will repel ants also, so a mint spray will work around the foundation or wherever they are entering.

Talk to your neighbors when they complement you on your gardens. Explain that yes you are growing a wide variety of plants so that you can attract a wide variety of birds and insects rather than just a few. Share the triumphs you have had by doing this—perhaps you don't see the slug infestations that they have in their yards because you have employed so many birds and insects to help eat those slugs. Or maybe the new butterflies you have seen in your garden are there because of the rain garden plants you have put in. This may cause your neighbors to think about growing some of the same plants and using similar methods that seem to work for you. In this way, you can build insect corridors in your neighborhood. This allows the good bugs to get from one infestation of food to the next. Those connections matter. They increase the health of the good bugs throughout the entire system. You will also see birds using these connections.

It is amazing how, if you give nature a little help, she can turn around almost any pest problem you have. It all is about making your outdoor space unattractive to the pests you don't want and very attractive to the life forms you do want—including your family, friends, and pets. If you can "fill" the space with good bugs and helpful birds, there is much less space for the problem pests.

Seemingly Scary or Bad Insects That Are Really Beneficial in Your Garden

ANTS: They eat lots of weed seeds, aerate the soil, and clean away some of the dead insects and birds. Ants may also milk aphids. If you see them on plants look for aphids. They are a clue for the gardener.

BEETLES: Most beetles are beneficial. They eat lots of other insects and clean up dead insects and birds. They are also good at aerating the soil.

BEES: They may sting and buzz noisily and can seem scary, but most are shy and gentle and just want to do their business of gathering nectar and pollen for their colony or their young. If a honey bee stings you, she will die. The stinger usually gets stuck in your skin and, when the bee tries to pull away, it rips out of the abdomen—making stinging you a last resort. Most native bees and bumblebees can sting you many times, but they seldom sting at all unless you threaten them.

CATERPILLARS: Many of these insects turn into beautiful, gentle butterflies or moths. All are a favorite food for adult birds to feed to their young. Young birds need high-protein diets and caterpillars are the perfect food.

EARWIGS: They look scary but really are not. Earwigs eat decaying organic matter, breaking it down even further. Usually, they don't bother plants unless their numbers are very high or other food sources are very low.

SLUGS: These sometimes can be a problem on hostas. Pull back the mulch and, if needed, use iron phosphate to kill them. Skunks and snakes eat a lot of slugs. Some birds will too. If you usually have a slug problem, before you expect them, lay down boards in the evening. In the morning, scrape the slugs hiding under them into the trash or out on the driveway for the birds to enjoy. They can increase in numbers exponentially, so be very proactive. Once your garden is diverse and healthy, you may want to leave mulch in place, as it will be the home of many beetles that can help keep slug populations in check. Invite birds in with bird baths or other water features.

TOMATO HORNWORMS: These are the larval stage of the sphinx or hawk moth and are devastating to your tomato crop. You can handpick the hornworms.

WASPS AND HORNETS: Often confused with bees, they are not "hairy" and they have a waist between their abdomen and thorax. Wasps and hornets are more territorial than bees and will protect their nest and young—and can sting more than once doing so. When frightened, they emit a pheromone that warns the entire colony of an impending attack. If you are stung, leave the area as quickly and quietly as possible. The female wasps are the ones that sting; the males do not. As long as you can leave their nests alone, they usually leave you alone too. If a nest is in a high-traffic area, you may need to remove it, but if it is far up in a tree or in another out-of-the-way place, you may be able to leave it alone. Wasps will also be more aggressive in late summer and early fall.

5

ORGANIC INSECT CONTROL

Four-lined plant bug nymph

Gardeners are forever on the lookout for "bad" bugs. We know that early spring brings sawfly larvae on our jack pines and other pines. Then our beautiful plants are beset with spittlebugs. Midsummer will find us battling Japanese beetles, flea beetles, cucumber beetles, tomato hornworms, aphids, scale—and the list goes on. Fall finds us trying to prevent Asian lady beetles and box elder bugs from moving into our homes. Winter may find us dealing with scale, mealybugs, or spider mites on our indoor houseplants. Every season brings new pests to "bug" us and our gardens. Just when we think we are safe, the next infestation appears. We have our ideal landscape in mind and it seems the insects are determined to destroy that. Trust me—this is not their goal. They simply want to survive and procreate. To deal with insects, we must learn to think like them.

Insects act and react in predictable ways and we can use that to our advantage. Say you are a cucumber beetle. Where will find your food and mates and lay eggs? Well, where all the cucumber plants are, of course. So, consider two yards next to each other. Both are beautifully landscaped. One has a delightful vegetable garden in the back, far from the house. It is well maintained, usually. The other has edibles mixed into all the plantings around the foundation and border gardens, even the pots and containers. All plants are the same in both yards, just arranged differently. Now, if you are that cucumber beetle, which yard would you find easier to live in? Probably the one with the vegetable garden out back—all the cucumber plants are in one place, they are a little out of the way and so see less foot traffic, and, with no trees or shrubs around, it is unlikely that predator birds will perch nearby to see the delicious cucumber beetles. Any other predatory insect would have a harder time crossing the wide-open lawn to reach the garden, even though there may be a wealth of bugs there to eat. Even if the predatory insect arrived there and ate all the insects, where would it lay its eggs for future generations?

PLANTING STRATEGIES

You can see that if you think like an insect you can outwit them. It is easy to hide our desired plants in our landscapes. One way is to hide the susceptible plants in plain sight: by planting plants all around them that the would-be pests don't want. For example, to protect your vegetable garden from deer, consider surrounding them with ornamental grasses that the deer don't want to eat. If you have lettuces that the rabbits would love, border them with fragrant herbs that disguise the smell of the lettuces and don't attract the rabbits. In addition to providing protection, using plants in this way can add a wonderful diversity to our landscapes. Another strategy is to welcome in all the predatory insects for that particular problem insect—for more on that, see Chapter 4.

Use floating row covers (polyspun white fabric) to cover the plants until they blossom and are, hopefully, beyond infestation time. Remove the covers to allow the pollinators in to pollinate the flowers so you get the cucumbers. Admittedly these floating row covers may not be the most attractive part of your landscape, but you may only need them when you concentrate the plants for the pest or plant all your susceptible plants in one place. Even if you need or want to cover the scattered plants in your landscape, it can be a point of discussion with your neighbors (why do you have all that white stuff covering some of your plants?) and will be a short-lived look for your garden. This is your third option.

A fourth option is timing. Because cucumber beetles, for example, are usually found in early to midsummer, wait until midsummer to plant them, if you can. You can protect the young plants from the beetles and, by the time they start to bloom, the beetles are done for the year; if they are not, the population of predatory insects is now much higher, having enjoyed all the earlier beetles in other yards, and can move to your connected yard now and continue to eat cucumber beetles.

SAWFLIES

Every spring, these insects appear on your pines, azaleas, or other shrubs. The female sawfly last year laid her eggs in the soft new needles. She has a saw-like apparatus on her abdomen called an ovipositor (just like the apple maggot fly!) that she pokes into the needle and lays the eggs. Next spring the eggs hatch. It is a creepy experience the first time you find these larvae on the pines. As you walk by the larvae—they look like worms or caterpillars—all seem to move at one time, reacting to your presence. The wonderful thing, though, is they will only eat the needles they were born on—they don't touch the new tender needles. So, your pine will not be stripped bare. That is good if you, the gardener, are not aware of the issue and allow it to continue. However, the larvae will pupate and they will mate and the females will lay eggs in the new soft needles. If your pine deals with major needle loss year after year, eventually it will die—but you can break the cycle easily.

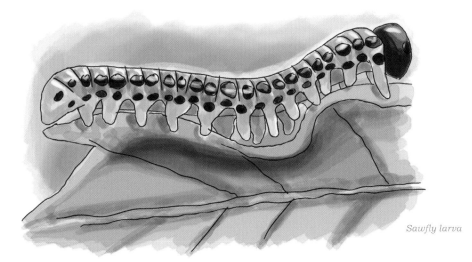

Sawfly larva

Because the larvae don't move around that much, it is easy to knock them from the pine when they are young (½ inch or smaller) with a strong stream of water. They can't climb back up on the tree and will die from hunger. No future generation will be had from them. You don't even have to use a soap or pesticide—just simple water. If the larvae are 1 inch, they are nearing pupation and, even when knocked down, may still pupate. In this case, a simple spray of insecticidal soap may help knock back the population, or wait until next year and act more quickly. Now, some people may get rid of their pines because of this possible annual infestation, but, really, is it too much work to give the tree or shrub a quick shower once a year?

For sawfly larva on other shrubs, you can hand pick them or spray them off also. Those on the azalea will strip the shrub bare if you let them; a healthy plant can recover, but you don't want the plant to have to grow two sets of leaves every year, so hand picking or spraying is a good option. These larvae can be harder to find than those on pines, as they are green and match the leaves in color. The life cycle for each sawfly may be slightly different, so you need to know which shrub they are on and then when they are most susceptible to your intervention. Often this is when they are very young, so be watchful for the infestation each year. Cleaning up under the shrub may reduce some of the larvae that fall and pupate under the shrub to turn into sawflies the next growing season. But if you catch the larvae before they pupate you can break the cycle and reduce future infestations in coming years. Know that the females can still fly in from other locations.

Your plan of action for sawflies: Be prepared one week before you think the larvae will emerge. Act quickly when you see them—spray them off the tree or shrub. Keep your plant healthy so it can recover from any feeding stress that occurred. Do not further stress the tree or shrub with improper pruning or cause any root damage and mitigate drought stress with supplemental water as appropriate.

Dangerous and Invasive Pests to Watch for and Report

GYPSY MOTH: Report sightings, remove egg masses from furniture, learn quarantine areas, and respect rules.

EMERALD ASH BORER: Report sightings, learn quarantine areas, never move firewood or fresh-cut lumber.

ASIAN LONG-HORNED BEETLE: Inspect trees for damage, report the pest, don't move firewood, diversify the tree varieties in your yard. The damage will be small oval areas on the bark of the trees where the female has removed the bark and laid her egg. The exit holes will be round and large enough to insert a pencil into. There may be frass, or sawdust-like product coming out of some of the holes or in piles under the holes on the ground.

ASIAN CITRUS PSYLLID: Learn quarantine areas, don't move homegrown fruit, use certified vendors or sellers of citrus fruit if in quarantine areas, don't move the pest out, inspect clothing.

GIANT AFRICAN SNAIL: Report if seen, call the USDA; don't handle without gloves as they can carry a parasite that causes meningitis.

SPOTTED WING DROSOPHILA: Identify the pest, report it, harvest fruit frequently, clean up ripe fruit. You will find the pest in the form of tiny maggots in the fruit. So, you would pick a bowl of berries and after they sit for a few moments you may notice they seem to move, when opened you will find the tiny maggots inside.

SPITTLEBUGS

Another pest that seems to really bother people is the spittlebug. It actually looks like spit on the plants. These insects do suck nutrition from your plants, usually flowers with soft stems, but seldom do any major damage. They create a wall of spit bubbles around them that protects them from insect and bird predation. This also protects them from any pesticide you may use to get rid of them. (An exception is a systemic like Systemic Insect Control by Bonide. Note that not all systemics will list spittle bugs. So, you must read the label and make sure that the pesticide is labeled to also treat for spittlebugs.

So, what's a gardener do? Well, realize the look may be gross, but they usually don't cause much damage. If you just can't stand it or the numbers seem high and your plants show signs of stress, again, a strong stream of water works to dislodge most of them and end the damage.

The plan of action with spittlebugs: Do nothing unless populations are high. If needed, spray them off with a strong stream of water.

JAPANESE BEETLES

The infestation of Japanese beetles has been advancing steadily westward. There really is no stopping the beetle infestations from moving, but you can limit the damage done. I was once approached by a woman who said her neighbor's garden had Japanese beetles the previous year. As a result, she was going to remove her rosebush to prevent them from coming into her yard. That is her right and option, but there are a few things she might have considered before such drastic action. How much does she love that rosebush? If it is a vital part of the landscape, there is no reason to remove it. If she doesn't really like it then, fine, remove it and replace it with something else. Also to be considered is what else in the landscape may attract the beetles? They also love raspberry, *Pelargonium* (better known as the common geranium, which is a wonderful trap plant for them—it acts like a drug and they stay right there), linden trees, grapes, apples, Virginia Creeper, Birch, Japanese and Norway maple, apricot, cherry, plum trees, pole beans, and other plants

Japanese beetles

too. Yours could become quite a sparse landscape if you tried to remove all the plants that Japanese beetles eat.

Next: How bad was the infestation in the neighbor's yard? Japanese beetle populations vary from year to year, especially if they are knocked back by late frosts. They begin their lives as grubs in the soil. The adult female can lay up to sixty eggs during her two-month life as an adult. The eggs are laid in summer and by fall are about 1 inch long. As the soil cools below 60°F, they move deeper for the winter. They re-emerge the next May when soil temperatures reach 50°F and begin to feed on grass roots. They also feed on strawberry, corn, and bean plant roots. Then they pupate and emerge as adult beetles in mid-June to begin feeding.

Japanese beetles have been known to feed on more than three hundred different plants. That is a lot of plants to lose from your landscape to avoid the beetles. Since most of us don't live near fields of strawberries or corn or beans, most of our beetles come from turf areas—and not necessarily your turf, as they can fly quite a distance. So, we don't need to destroy our lawns either.

If you know that Japanese beetles are an issue for your garden, begin looking for the scouts—the early emerging adults—about one week before you would expect to see them. When you find the beetles, early in the morning while still chilled from the cool night and not as quick to fly away, knock them into a bucket of soapy water and they will drown. Keep doing this every day, as long as you can, or every evening when it is cooler. If you can knock back the first wave of scouts you will greatly reduce the later damage to your garden. Japanese beetles emit a pheromone that attracts other beetles and their feeding on the plants' leaves also emits a fragrance from the damaged leaves that attracts other beetles. Do not use a Japanese beetle trap. This uses the same pheromone to attract beetles and will draw more beetles to your yard.

If you do have a large infestation on, say, your raspberry plants and have a large yard, you may want to try a trap at the far end of the yard to draw them away from the raspberries. Know that most plants recover from their feeding. If it's your precious rosebush, cover it with a floating row cover to minimize the chance of the beetles getting to the bush—but you will probably be covering it in full bloom, the most beautiful time, and also when pollinators are most active around it. This could be an option one year when you just can't do anything else.

Draw in some birds to help with the Japanese beetle problem. Some have noticed that starlings are starting to eat the beetles. It sometimes takes a few years for the local bird population to add new insects to its diet. Include some birdbaths near the beetle population to draw the birds in. They may become helpers in your quest to be beetle free.

If you are going to treat the Japanese beetle grubs, time your application of pesticide carefully. Mid to late summer, as the eggs hatch, is the time the larvae are most susceptible. Make sure to use the correct product and use it according to the instructions. You may want to consider this a last resort as many other soil-dwelling insects may be killed or hurt and that could be reflected in the future health of your garden.

Your Japanese beetle action plan: Know which plants they want to eat. Grow a healthy lawn that includes many beetles and birds to eat the larvae as they feed or emerge and, if you wish, reduce the size of your lawn if appropriate. Time your plan of action. Be prepared before they arrive to knock back the population from the beginning. Use their pheromones against them. Bring in natural predators, such as birds, to assist you. If you are dealing with a huge infestation year after year or are finding your orchard of apple trees at risk, use a prescribed pesticide for the grubs at the proper stage of development. Understand this will kill the current Japanese beetle grubs but not prevent more from flying in next season.

APHIDS

Aphids are soft-bodied insects. Sometimes in warmer climates they may be an almost year-round pest. In colder climates, they don't usually overwinter but are blown on the winds from the south to enjoy the feasts in our yards. They are insects with sucking mouthparts, so that is the damage they cause: they bite into the plant and suck out the nutrition, which is usually concentrated sugars in the sap. This is the nutrition that the plant needs for its own use, so it can injure the health of the plant if too much is lost to sucking insects. They need soft stems or branches to feed on and as we overfertilize our perennial plants we cause a flush of soft, lush growth in spring along with the emerging tender leaves, and the aphids are in food heaven. You can easily wash the aphids from your plants with a strong stream of water, or use insecticidal soaps, or let the population grow enough to attract the predators that love aphids, namely those we call ladybugs. Most of us know what the adult ladybug looks like and, yes, the adults do eat some aphids. It is the larvae stage of the ladybug, however, that is the most voracious eater of aphids. These youngsters look nothing like the adults. To me, they look a bit like alligators—tiny hungry alligators on the leaves of the plants looking for aphids. This is another reason we really need to know *which* bug we see before we react and kill it. In the case of ladybugs, you likely would never connect the adult with the larvae—there is no family resemblance at all.

In an effort to speed the process of getting the predator insects into the garden, some gardeners purchase ladybugs from the nursery or online. If you do this, read and follow the instructions. The timing of their release is important. They also need to be sprayed with sugar water to limit their flying away and, as sensible as it sounds, there needs to be enough of an aphid population to keep them fed long enough to mate and lay eggs. If you release the ladybugs in the heat of the day, where there are few aphids, and don't spray them with sugar water, the odds are that most of them will fly away. Often, they may not find any food and die. Sometimes it works to help nature along; sometimes it does not. Only you can judge the damage being done by aphid feeding, your plants' health and response to the feeding, your tolerance for the damage, and the time it will take for the predator insects to come in and help.

Every year the Skyline honey locust out on the boulevard is hit with honey locust aphids. Yes, sometimes aphids prefer one plant over all others.

Aphids

It gets these aphids every year for a number of reasons. The honey locust tree is one of the last trees to leaf out in spring. This way it avoids the late frosts common in my state, but it also means, by the time it is warm and the winds have brought the hungry aphids from the south, the leaves are tiny and tender. Even though this is a tough boulevard tree (which is why it was planted by my city), the aphids do affect it. Because I don't use pesticides on the tree or in my landscape, hopefully the predator bugs can get a good meal in the tree. This is a moderate-sized tree and the garden hose will not spray a strong enough stream of water to dislodge many of the aphids. So, I must rely on the tree to defend itself. I can help by growing a great native or semi-native garden under the tree that will attract a variety of insects and birds. I don't prune the tree at the wrong time and don't stress the tree with a lot of digging to disturb the roots. The tree is quite healthy despite this yearly aphid infestation. Sometimes you just have to let nature take its course.

Every year the *Rudbeckia* plants in my garden are covered with red aphids. The plants do okay and I either spray off the aphids with water or squish them with my fingers. The red aphids seem to want this one plant at this one time of the season.

Your plan for dealing with aphids: Decide how much damage you and the plant can stand before you step in. Let the predator insects do their job. If you must get involved, spray the plant with a strong stream of water. Resort to insecticidal soap if you find the aphid population is out of control. Use the soap early in the morning, testing it on a few leaves the day before to be sure it won't burn the plants, which is another stressor you don't want to add to the mix. Never spray the insecticidal soap on the plant when it is in bright sunshine or when pollinators are present.

APPLE MAGGOT FLIES

Another insect to consider is the apple maggot fly. This fly is similar to the sawfly adult in that the female also has an ovipositor on her abdomen. However, the apple maggot fly lays her eggs in the ripening apples. The maggots hatch, eat tunnels through the apples, work their way out, and fall to

the ground. They pupate and overwinter in the soil under the tree, emerging the following year to begin the cycle again. The apples are still edible, but not very attractive with the brown trails throughout and the dimpled skin—the result of the pokes of the ovipositor.

If you have apple maggots, you have options to work with. The female fly is attracted to the red ripening apples. These are the places she wants to lay her eggs. You can use traps to determine when the fly is in the area. These sticky traps can be anything red, a croquet ball, a holiday ornament, or even the trap balls sold for this purpose. Apply Tanglefoot or another sticky product meant to attract and trap the flies—to the ball trap. I suggest wrapping the red trap in plastic wrap or a plastic sandwich bag and applying the sticky trap substance to the wrap. It is easier to clean rather than scraping the used sticky bug-filled mess off the ball. You use this trap just to determine when the insects are present. As soon as the female fly shows up on your traps—the red color of the ripening apples attracts her more than the green or slight red—proceed to whatever next step you have decided upon.

You can, at this time, begin a regimen of insecticidal fruit tree sprays. You will need to apply these sprays every seven to ten days as instructed for about four weeks, or longer—as long as the flies are present. Follow the label instructions.

You can also try an organic spray of kaolin clay. This spray covers the entire plant—leaves, fruit, and branches—with a layer of clay. The fly can't penetrate the clay to deposit her eggs. You may need to reapply this clay if rain or heavy dew washes it off.

The final option is to bag the apples. To do this, use sandwich bags that zip shut. The number of apples you want to harvest is the number of bags you need. Cut off the two lower corners of each bag, which allows moisture to drain from the bag and minimizes rotting fruit. Bag the apples as soon as you can, when they are quite small—the size of a marble or even smaller. (If done soon enough, this may also deter the plum curculio, a weevil that lays its eggs soon after the fruit starts to develop. The female pokes her ovipositor into the fruit and lays the eggs, which causes rough, tan-colored patches on the fruit. It is mostly cosmetic in damage but can look unappetizing. The bags also protect the apples from birds or even squirrels.)

As you bag each apple you want to protect, thin the crop so each apple has plenty of room to grow. Leaving 6 inches or more between apples is recommended. It may look funny and people may ask what you are doing, but you will get a pest-free harvest in a few months for just a few hours work. Pick up any windfall apples— this is normal, as the tree drops some fruit in June—and clean up all fallen fruit and other debris from under the tree to minimize further pest problems.

LEAFMINERS

Often these insects are found in columbine leaves, but that is not the only plant they will attack. These tiny insects can live between the layers of the leaf where they eat their way through the leaf, creating wandering brown trails. The simplest way to deal with these is to remove the leaf as soon as you notice the trail and either toss it in the trash or send it to the city compost (if available) where the heat will kill the insect. The damage done is mostly superficial and this insect is not really a big problem.

FOUR-LINED PLANT BUGS

These bugs, with their scraping mouthparts, scrape off the top layer of the leaf, leaving behind a small round wound that turns black quite quickly. You may see the damage as little black pinhead-sized dots on the upper leaves of some plants. These bugs seem to be attracted to plants that don't normally have a lot of pests, such as mints, rhubarb, chrysanthemum, and many native prairie plants. Usually we consider prairie plants quite pest free, but four-lined plant bugs can attack many of them. The damage can look quite bad.

These insects begin as small, red, fast-moving nymphs. As adults, they have green or black stripes alternating with yellow running the length of their body, hence the name four-lined plant bug. There is usually only one generation per year, so feeding time is limited to early summer to midsummer, allowing the plants to recover well. You can spray the red soft-bodied nymphs with insecticidal soap but, as this is a contact poison and the insects move quickly, is it not very effective. Some gardeners stand over their plants and "clap" the leaves where they see the insects, squishing them. The easiest way I know to deal with them is to remove the aboveground parts of the affected plants at the end of the growing season. The adults have laid eggs in the woody bases of these plants so removing the stems will reduce the population next year.

SCALE

Scale—a small sucking insect—is one insect that may cause you to remove a plant or resort to a systemic pesticide. When young, they are called crawlers and are mobile. At this stage, they are susceptible to insecticidal soap and bird and insect predation. Once adults, they form a hard shell that they hide under and proceed to suck nutrition from the plant. This shell protects them from contact poisons and may prevent birds from taking them. You can pry them off, or rub each scale insect with cotton swabs dipped in alcohol. As you can imagine, these are time-consuming and probably not very effective responses.

You may need, or want, to resort to a systemic pesticide labeled for this use. Systemic pesticides are often granules

Scale

watered into the soil where they are absorbed by the plant. The poison is carried throughout the entire plant, making the whole thing poison to whatever insect nibbles on it. This is one way to save your plant, as a scale infestation is often the death of it. Once the systemic is in the plant, it remains active as long as is noted on the label. This may be an entire growing season or longer. Because the poison is throughout the entire plant, it will be found in the flowers, leaves, pollen, nectar, and roots and stems. *Never* use a systemic on any food plant. Always read, understand, and follow all label instructions. The pest and the plant must be listed on the label.

SQUASH VINE BORERS

These insects fly in and lay eggs right in the stem of the plant where it emerges from the ground. As the borer hatches, it proceeds to eat the inside of the stem, stopping nutrients from flowing from leaves to roots or roots to leaves. The entire vine wilts quickly and dies. This insect can be misidentified by the gardener as the plant just needing more water. By the time the gardener realizes it, the plant is dead.

There are many easy ways around this pest. Plant your squash a few weeks later and use floating row covers to protect them until they begin to flower. By that time, you may have missed the time when the female adult is flying around laying eggs. Remove the floating row cover to allow for pollination. You can also plant your squash as usual, but wrap the stems with a bit of aluminum foil. This may prevent the female from laying her eggs. Grow butternut squash. This variety has a thicker-skinned stem that the vine borer does not seem to be able to penetrate to lay her eggs. Another option is to plant Hubbard squash, which is extremely attractive to the vine borer and can be used as a trap crop.

You can also plant your favorite squash plants and remain vigilant. Inspect the base of the plant frequently and, as the plant vine grows, bury a part of it so it roots into the soil as it grows. Do this a number of times as the plant continues to vine.

Damage from vine borers may be mistaken for dehydration. If your squash is wilting, check the bases of the stems for eggs.

If the vine borer does lay eggs in the original base of the plant, cut the remaining plant away from the base and it should be okay to use the roots it has put down along the vine. If you notice the plant is wilting and know it is the vine borer, cut the stem open, remove the borer (it looks like a fat worm or grub), bury the stem with soil, and water well. The vine may recover.

If you have any other borers, such as lilac or dogwood, or any other borers in your shrubs, or iris borer in the iris bed, treat them the same way. First, though, make sure it is borer damage. Borers often are found only on certain plants. Know the plant you are dealing with and, if borers are a problem, your research will identify the borer and the best time to treat it. Can you protect the crucial area from infestation to begin with by using some kind of barrier? Can you limit the damage by removing the infested part and keep the rest of the plant healthy? Can you remove the borer (such as the iris borer) and save the plant?

As you can see, many "pest" insects can be dealt with fairly easily if we know the insect and learn to think like it does. Anticipate what it will do and you can outmaneuver just about any insect. So many times, if we mimic nature with all her resources, we find balance can be achieved quickly and pest populations kept down by many other facets of our outdoor spaces.

ORGANIC AND HUMANE ANIMAL CONTROL

6

Animal pests can be quite devastating to our gardens. They can eat our plants to the ground, they can debark our trees and shrubs, they can eat our vegetable garden crops or the fruit we are trying to grow. In addition, they can dig while looking for other food like grubs and worms and cause holes in our lawns. Some disturb the soil around our plants so that the plants perish. Some animals are underground and eat the plants roots— again this will kill the plants. Some damage is only cosmetic and we can let it be.

Birds are generally a welcome sight in the yard, but they can also be a nuisance. Planting strategically helps focus them on eating only the things you want eaten.

RABBITS

Rabbits are probably one of the most frequently complained-about pests. These animals can be active during the day but are more active at night. In fact, that is one way to determine that rabbits are doing the damage. (When does it happen? At night? Probably rabbits. Squirrels, by contrast, are active during the day.)

Rabbits may sometimes leave behind distinctive round marble-shaped pellets of rabbit feces, but will often ingest their feces so their digestive tract can absorb the nutrients missed the first time.

Rabbits are herbivores. Their teeth continue to grow, so they often gnaw and chew on twigs and branches along with eating many of our plants. During winter, they can girdle trees and kill them. They will also eat many shrubs to the ground during cold winter months. Protect the trees and shrubs with fencing or repellents labeled to protect against rabbits. If you are starting a garden, install the fencing as soon as you are done planting. Once installed, the rabbits may leave your garden alone but, if they have found food there and you try to fence it off, they may work very hard to get under or through the fence.

During summer, usually, full-grown plants face no danger from rabbits. During spring, the young rabbits can squeeze through regular rabbit fencing and will sample and eat many plants that their parents would not touch. Baby bunnies just aren't smart enough, yet, to know which plants they should eat and which plants they should not. Usually, strongly fragrant or strong-tasting plants are not what the rabbits prefer. This means most of our herbs will be safe, as will many of our more pungent flowers. But newly emerging plants or mild-smelling flowers, such as crocus, are delicious to rabbits—and they see those emerging plants before we ever do, right there at ground level. We don't pay as close attention to our gardens as the animals and that is why they often get to the plants before we can protect them or just before we pick that almost-ripe fruit or vegetable.

Rabbits are usually solitary and territorial, but can have territories that overlap or be seen in groups cavorting as part of the mating ritual. They are very common in our urban landscapes. We have managed landscapes—bushes and shrubbery and other protected spots, such as decks and porches, for them to live and raise their young. We provide easy-to-find buffets and have limited predators. No wonder their populations are so high.

As mentioned, fencing is the best way to prevent the rabbits from even starting on your plants and gardens, but sometimes that is not possible or practical. As an alternative, you can grow plants they don't like, such as herbs, tougher grasses, and sedges. You can also plant clover in the lawn, which may distract them from your garden, as they really do enjoy clover.

Many of the repellants discussed in Chapter 3 will work to some extent. Blood meal, synthetic repellents, and animal urine like fox urine along with homemade repellants containing eggs or garlic will work. Change these up every two to four weeks. Reapply as needed depending upon weather and precipitation. Don't spray directly on food crops unless labeled for this use.

Planting the plants the rabbits don't want thickly around the perimeter of your garden may help too. But these must be thick enough to discourage rabbits from pushing through them to get the plants inside. Planting a row of marigolds around the outside of your garden 6 or 10 inches apart after the plants inside have started to come up will not work—first because the rabbits already know there is food inside the garden, and second because the marigolds are too far apart to present a physical or fragrance barrier.

CHIPMUNKS

I admit it. These little rodents are cute and I love to hear their chirps and watch them scurry through the yard. However, they can be a pest for many gardeners. Because they are solitary, making your yard unhospitable to them may remedy the problem.

Chipmunks are omnivorous and will eat worms, grubs, nuts, fruit, tender plant starts, and seeds. They do help keep down insect problems and weeds from sprouting everywhere. But they also dig and they do that extensively. Their burrows can be up to 11 feet long and have many entrances. They tend to dig in soft soils of freshly planted containers and newly planted vegetable garden beds.

Chipmunks like to use low shrubs or dead trees for cover.

Excluding them can be difficult because although they are mostly ground-dwelling animals they can climb over fencing if need be. You will see them in your yard and garden if they are there because they are active during the day. That can make it easier to identify the source of the damage.

Birds don't mind hot pepper flakes, but they will deter squirrels and chipmunks from snacking on your birdseed.

To protect newly planted containers, try repellents that use strong-smelling ingredients—garlic, rotten eggs, spices, or other substances. If your containers are growing food for your family, make sure the repellent is labeled for food crops. You can use these in the vegetable gardens when planting your plants or seeds. Some people use hardware cloth over the newly planted seed rows. This will stop the chipmunks from digging directly to the seeds and, unless they are very hungry, they will probably find another food source. Remove the hardware cloth as soon as the danger has passed and the seeds sprout.

You may find the spilled seeds from your bird feeder keep the little rodents satisfied enough so they don't bother the rest of your gardens. In fall, you will see the chipmunks repeatedly stuffing their cheeks full of seeds and nuts. They store these in their cache and eat them during the winter months. If you prefer not to encourage the rodents and still feed the birds, consider adding hot pepper flakes to your birdseed. There are mixes sold with hot pepper flakes already added. They are more expensive and so, as I am a frugal gardener, I add my own first to see if they work. The birds don't seem to mind the hot fiery taste and yet it is usually not preferred by mammals such as chipmunks or squirrels.

Some people spray their containers or woody plants with hot pepper sprays. If you find the chipmunks chewing on the containers or the bark of shrubs (it could be rabbits or squirrels too), determine when the damage is occurring. During the night? The chipmunks and squirrels are not the culprits (think skunks or rabbits). Clean the containers first—you may have handled them and left "good smells" on them—and apply the repellent as directed.

As with any repellent, those that use odors or tastes need to be reapplied when they become ineffective or after heavy rains, a long period of hot weather, or heavy dews. Many repellents are less effective in cold weather. Read the label for this information.

Because they are small creatures, chipmunks prefer the cover of bushes, tall grasses, and shrubs. They are easy prey out in the open for hawks, so, if you remove their cover and encourage the predators, your problem with chipmunks can be solved. Leaving dead trees standing as snags for the raptors to sit on during the day and watch for prey is a good way to invite them into your ecosystem. Make sure, though, that those dead trees are in areas where when they fall they will not damage people, animals, or property. Some cities or associations may not allow these trees to stand. Always follow the legal restrictions for your area. Those raptors will be just as happy to take the songbirds you attract to your yard with the bird feeders, so make sure you provide the correct cover for the birds you bring in.

Free-roaming cats may also take care of any chipmunk problem you have. They do help keep down the rodents—chipmunk, mice, and vole populations along with some squirrels, but they also kill many of our endangered songbirds. However, it is not legal in most areas to let your cat roam free. Free-roaming cats may be killed by coyote, wolves, dogs, and cars and usually have a much shorter life than their fellow housebound felines.

Because chipmunks are prey animals they may react strongly to the smell of blood. Sprinkle blood meal (see page 52) around the area you want the chipmunks to avoid. Because it is a powder, you need to reapply it after heavy rains or dews or watering. Again, follow label directions. If you have a dog or the area is open to neighborhood dogs you may find them attracted to the area. This is another good reason to keep your pets contained on your property or your dog on a leash when off your property—you don't know who is putting down what in their yards and gardens. Protect your pets and keep them safe. It helps keep the neighbors happy too.

GOPHERS

These small rodents live in tunnels in our lawns and gardens and can do lots of damage by eating the roots of our plants. They seldom venture far from their tunnels, so you may not see them aboveground very often. Their natural predators include dogs, cats, snakes, and raptors. You may be able to use some repellents against them, but it is hard if not impossible to get them into the underground spaces where the gophers will be bothered by them. Traps will work; you will need to rehome the animal to a safe location where it will not impact other homeowners. Fencing can be helpful, but you need to dig down 2 feet into the ground for your fence to be an effective barrier, and this may not be doable for many people. Removing cover near their tunnel entrances and being in the area frequently may make them uncomfortable enough to move on. If you have special plants that you want to protect, you can plant them in wire baskets—¼- to ½-inch hardware cloth will work. This will create a barrier so the animals can't get to the roots of the plants. They will not eat daffodil and most allium (onion and garlic) plants.

SQUIRRELS

Squirrels are a frequent nuisance for anyone with a bird feeder.

Another common pest is the squirrel. They may be as much, or even more, complained about as the rabbits. Squirrels are common in urban areas—perhaps too common. They are clever creatures with extensive memories. It is this memory that may make it a better deal for us to get along with them and "train" them rather than remove them.

Squirrels are very territorial. When we dig in their territory they are extremely interested. That is why they dig into just-planted containers, dig up your just-planted plants, and remove your tulip bulbs. This is their territory. You must be cleverer than they are.

When you dig, try to disguise the freshly dug soil or containers. Use a mulch to cover the surface after you water in the plants or put down a barrier over those freshly planted

When planting or watering bulbs, hide the squirrel-attracting smell of freshly dug soil by covering it with mulch. Herbal tea and other scents are also good options, as discussed on page 53.

tulip bulbs. You can also use repellents based on smell that will cover the smell of newly installed tulip bulbs. Dip the bulbs into the repellent and let them dry a bit before planting as usual. Even if the sight and smell of the freshly turned soil interests the squirrels, they may ignore it due to the less-than-attractive other smells they sense. You can use a similar method when planting new perennials and annuals that may be subject to squirrel relocation. Just spritz the soil around the plants. If you are planting edible plants, make sure the product is labeled for use on food plants.

Another way to hide your digging is to use a fragrant mulch, such as cocoa shell. *Do not* use this mulch if dogs are in the area. Dogs should not ingest this mulch as it may kill them. Use this only in a thin layer as it molds quickly. When it does mold just fluff it up—the mold is natural as the cocoa decomposes. Once the smell of freshly dug soil has settled the squirrels will ignore the plants and containers—at least until fall when they decide the friable (loose) soil makes a great place to bury acorns and walnuts.

Squirrels also like digging in compost piles or bins. Don't worry about them. Consider them helpers in your quest for compost as they turn and aerate it for you.

Many times, in early summer, I hear many questions about trees. They seem to be dropping all kinds of small branches and leaves. People are concerned their trees are sick or have some kind of insect pest. This usually is not the case—it is squirrels. They are simply clearing their tree limb runways of new growth and keeping water sprouts (those upward growing branches found on established branches and limbs) to a minimum.

Squirrels are part of our urban landscape. They can be a challenge to deal with, but we can co-exist with them. If you feed the birds you may find that squirrels empty the feeders before the birds can get there. As with chipmunks (see page 98), purchase birdseed with hot pepper flakes added or add your own to the food. The squirrels will not enjoy the hot pepper and may leave your feeders alone. You can purchase squirrel-resistant bird feeders or those that use baffles. Even adding a slinky to the pole holding the feeder may work. The squirrel gets to where the slinky is attached to the pole and the slinky stretches down and the squirrel slides down the pole too.

Some people have problems with squirrels bothering their vegetable gardens. If squirrels are taking the tomatoes—eating one bite and leaving the rest on the patio or your front step—they are not taunting you. They are just thirsty and realize those tomatoes are not apples and are not solving their thirst. During growing season, provide the squirrels with a dish of fresh water. Remember to change it every two days or so to minimize mosquito issues. Keep this dish near your garden and the squirrel will probably leave those tomatoes for you to harvest. Try bagging the apples as you would for apple maggot flies (see page 90); that may prevent some being taken by squirrels.

Squirrels may seem to be troublemakers in our landscapes but they eat lots of seeds that then don't sprout into weeds. They trim our trees so we don't have to do as much pruning to keep branches from crossing; they aerate our soils and compost bins for us; they plant and, yes eat, a lot of walnuts and acorns that may grow into walnut trees or mighty oaks. And, if you take time to watch them, they can add a humorous aspect to almost any day in the garden.

DEER

Deer are mostly crepuscular or nocturnal—active at dawn and dusk, though they will often be active all night as well. During the day, they usually reside in protected shady areas, bed down, and stay quiet. When we understand the times of day they are most active, we can be more aware and watch for them.

Deer and auto crashes are common and cause millions of dollars in insurance claims each year. Because of the closer interaction of deer and human communities we have also seen an increase in Lyme disease and other diseases. (Due also to a better understanding, diagnosis, and reporting of the disease.) Lyme is transmitted by the deer tick, now known as the blacklegged tick, *Ixodes scapularis*, which is found on the deer and in their territory.

Deer are herd animals that have lost most natural predators. We have taken over much of the places they used to live and they have graciously allowed us to do so and try to live with us. They find our manicured landscapes, filled with tasty plants and free of many predators—except cars—to be quite acceptable. We have made many of our neighborhoods perfect deer habitats.

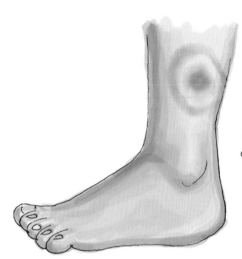

Deer usually travel their territory on specific trails at specific times. They keep the same schedule most of the time, so if you can disrupt their daily visit to your yard or garden they may bypass your area and bother others instead.

If you know where they enter your property, consider adding a fence there. It can be a sturdy 8-foot-tall fence or it can be a simple 5- to 7-foot temporary fence of deer netting. This netting is monofilament line (like fishing line), usually black in color, with ¾- to 1-inch squares. From a few feet away, it is not very visible. Since deer will not see it easily, they bump into it with their sensitive noses. Not seeing it clearly or being able to know what it is may be enough to cause them to change their route, as is the uncertainty of running into it on "their" path. They may also break through it but, because it is temporary, it can be put up again.

If there are deer in your area and you get an insect bite that develops a "bullseye" rash, get to the doctor right away—this is the telltale sign of a bite from a deer tick carrying Lyme disease. The bite may be accompanied by flulike symptoms.

If you have a larger open area where deer may enter, use a permaculture response. Plant a hedgerow of plants. Permaculture (a combination of "permanent" and "agriculture") is a way of gardening that looks at the whole system and all the parts and activities involved in that system. It is a way of working with nature and using what we learn to garden more easily—for example, "stacking" plant functions so that every plant creates more than one useful benefit. When using permaculture there is no waste, energy is recycled again and again, small changes are made when needed, and observation is important. While there is a lot that goes into this, basically it is working with nature and harnessing the systems of energy in nature to create a more sustainable and resilient outdoor space.

Animals are part of the whole picture and if you have an issue with deer you can consider what and how and where you plant to direct the deer around your yard. A deer-deterring hedgerow can be done in a number of ways. One way is to plant sacrificial plants on the outside of the hedge. The deer will eat these and be on their way. Plant thickly so they can't walk through the hedge. Plant your desired plants on the inside of the hedge. You can also plant thorny plants, such as raspberries or native plums, on the outside of the hedge. The deer may or may not eat them and, when planted closely, will not push through them. You can, if you want, also install a fence as an additional barrier between these two plants' lines. It only needs to be 4 or 5 feet tall. Deer are prey animals and rely on their senses of sight and smell to keep them safe. If they can't see through the area, they are unlikely to push through it—there could be a wolf, coyote, or other predator in there!

Of course, you can always plant plants' the deer don't eat—but if they are hungry enough they will graze on just about anything. By using what you know about the deer and their habits, you can gently redirect them away from your yard.

Another option is to create a hammock of bird netting or deer fencing that is just above the hostas, or other targeted plants, as they grow. As the deer lower their heads to snack on your plants, their noses hit the fencing instead and they don't get to the plants. If you leave this netting up during autumn when the leaves fall, they may fall in the netting, making it easier to toss them into the compost or grass to be cut with your mulching mower rather than raking the hosta beds.

Strategically planted hedgerows direct deer toward or away from certain areas of your property.

If you are not certain the damage is from deer, here are some signs:

- Deer usually pull plants out of the ground while eating them. This is common in newly planted plants.
- On shrubs and trees, the damage will have a shredded look to the cuts/bites. It will also be at deer height, rather than lower and clipped neatly as it would be with rabbit damage.
- You may also find deer droppings or evidence of them bedding down for the night or day.

You can use the deer's sense of smell against them by using repellents that feature strong-smelling ingredients. Deer learn to live in an urban environment and get used to human smells, so change it up. Use garlic for a while, then rotten eggs, then switch to a more chemical smell or fragrant bar soap. Urine from wolves and coyotes may work. Even the family dog may help in this battle simply by leaving its smell in your yard. The deer may not know the dog they sense is a tiny toy poodle, not a large guard dog.

Hiding your plants in plain sight works too (see pages 20 and 80). Plant susceptible, tasty plants near the house or in containers on the deck or balcony. Those planted farther away can be hidden by fragrant herbs planted around them, or by ornamental grasses. Deer don't seem to like to forage amongst the ornamental grasses for their food. Plant the grasses thickly near and around the plants you are protecting. It can be a beautiful addition to your landscape.

During spring and summer, deer browse mostly on tender plants and vegetables. In fall, they look for food with a higher fat or carbohydrate content to build their fat stores for winter. They prefer acorns, nuts, fruits, and other higher-calorie foods. Yes, they also enjoy the seeds from the bird feeder. So, clean up the acorns, pull the feeders at night, and pick up fallen fruit.

Deer also hear well and don't like loud noises or unexpected events. A radio left on a talk station may work. Change it up and let them listen to various stations to see which works best. A line of cans can cause a ruckus when

Simple white cloths hanging from a tree branch will deter some deer.

bumped—hang them near where the deer walk. As mentioned previously, you may also want to invest in a motion-activated sprinkler (just remember to turn it off during the day or you will get blasted too).

As prey animals, deer have a limited sense of sight, which you can use this against them. As discussed on page 56, hang 6- to 8-inch-long pieces of white cloth from fences or bushes about deer tail high to mimic the white flag of alarm that does use to warn others of danger. The white works well at dusk and in early dawn lighting.

During fall, the male deer begin the rut season, where they rub the velvet from their antlers on tree trunks and spar with other males for the right to mate or hold territory. This rubbing can damage tree bark, especially the tender bark of fruit trees or newly planted trees. Protect the trunks of these trees with a cylinder of hardware cloth around the trunk and up to the first branch. Using hardware cloth instead of paper tape or chicken wire will protect the tree from rabbit, vole, and mouse damage also.

During winter, the deer will still be actively browsing and eating in their territory. Now the food they will eat will be the bark of trees and shrubs, lichens, and the twigs and branches of trees they can reach. A favorite winter food will be your arborvitae (evergreen). Protect these plants with deer fencing over the shrubs, tall fencing to exclude the deer, or more repellents that focus on smell. You will need to reapply the repellents due to weather or time according to label directions. Granular products may last longer in cold temperatures.

Deer also love fruit tree twigs and branches during winter. Protect the trees with fencing—a ring of two or three fences they can't easily figure out how to jump over may work. Hanging repellents from tree branches may help as well as spraying with hot pepper spray. Remember, reapply these sprays frequently during winter.

Deer are ruminants—animals with a four-part stomach—so they can ingest and get nourishment from a wide variety of plant sources, many of which are harder to digest like bark and twigs and lichens. You may even want to give in and, if legal and it makes sense to you, provide corn or other food in a far-off location for the deer in your yard.

Motion-activated bright lights may deter them or make it uncomfortable for them to bed down in your yard. The resulting damage to your gardens and the feces they leave are reasons enough to encourage them to move on.

Be aware: You must know the legal ramifications of any action you take to hunt or physically remove deer from your property.

Raccoons are omnivores, so there are few things in the average yard they won't eat.

RACCOONS

The raccoon is another animal that seems to be a bother in our landscape. Raccoons can damage gardens and lawns and even homes and outbuildings. Raccoons are very intelligent. Studies show they can remember solutions to problems (such as how to get the trash can open) for up to three years—so keep the garbage area clean. Make sure you have tight-fitting lids on your trash cans. Also clean the outside of the cans to reduce the residual "good smells" that may attract the raccoons.

Raccoons are omnivores, so just about everything in your yard or garden is a potential target. They enjoy earthworms and grubs and beetles and other insects. In procuring them, they may dig horseshoe-shaped divots in turf areas. If you find holes or divots of turf in the morning that were not there yesterday, chances are a raccoon or two visited overnight. (Skunks are another possibility but the holes they leave are round.) You may want to thank the raccoons for eating the grubs that eat your grass roots. Just push the divots back into the surrounding soil; it should recover nicely.

Raccoons are nocturnal so, mainly, you will not see them unless you are out at night. There is some evidence that the black mask around their eyes, rather than just making them look cute, actually cuts down on glare and lets them see even better in low-light situations. At times, due to hunting for sparse food, they may also be active during the day.

In spring and early summer the raccoons usually concentrate on eating high-protein foods, such as insects, frogs, and eggs, sometimes even carrion. In fall, they rely more on high-calorie foods such as nuts and fruits. They need the extra calories for the winter months. This is the pattern for most animals, including birds.

If you decide to remove the raccoon, check with your local animal control or a professional. It may not be legal to trap and release somewhere else, or to trap and humanely kill the animal. In truth, the raccoon populations in our urban areas are so high that another will move in quickly to take its place. Relocating a territorial animal is not a humane response. They will have to fight for territory, be uncertain of food sources, and may be hurt fighting or die from starvation. That is not a humane outcome. Plus moving your problem to someone else's backyard is not a kind thing to do either.

Keep garbage areas neat and use secure lids, or racoons will have a field day.

Even though they have fewer predators, the average urban raccoon's lifespan is one to three years. With this in mind and remembering that the population may be quite dense, you can see that these animals will be a continuous "pest" for the average homeowner or gardener. Although they will remember the efforts you use to repel them, the next generations may not and will need to be instructed again by you.

What can you do? Clean up fallen fruit; don't leave pet food out overnight; take in bird feeders at night and feed only what can be eaten each day; lock up chickens at night. Raccoons have been known to break into hen houses to get eggs and, yes, kill chickens. They don't usually attack pets, but if cornered they may.

If afraid, the raccoon would prefer to run and climb to safety—easily climbing fences and trees. It may actually come down from trees head first.

Because they can climb, they may climb—using trees and fences—up on your roof and remove chimney caps or work their way into attics to den up with new kits. If this happens, remove them as quickly as you can, repair the damage, and close up the entrance. Remove any tree limbs that provided access. Use a professional to remove them or try a bright flashing strobe light or loud noises—either may encourage them to move on. Strong-smelling repellents may keep them from returning to that area.

Raccoons do carry rabies, so avoid contact with them. Do not feed raccoons or get them used to being around humans more than they already are. Usually, an infected raccoon will remain in its den, but not always. If raccoons have taken to using part of your yard or garden as a latrine this must be stopped quickly. Raccoon feces can carry many diseases, including roundworms and giardia, that are easily passed to humans or pets. Discourage them strongly from continuing to use the area using repellants, motion-activated water sprinklers, lights, or loose fencing that bends over when the raccoons try to climb up. If the area has been cleaned

Corn is a racoon favorite, but surrounding your plants with beans and squash using the "three sisters" strategy is a tried-and-true protective technique.

To prevent fish in your water feature from becoming a meal, be sure your pond has a protective overhang under which they can hide from predators.

properly and you can keep them away for a time, they probably will not return to this spot to use as a latrine. Make it as uncomfortable for them as you can.

You may want to hire a professional to clean up the feces and disinfect the area because it is hazardous. If you decide to do it yourself, contact your local animal control, professional, or extension office and get the correct information to do this safely. You will need protective clothing, special masks, disinfectant, and more.

Raccoons also enjoy our gardens and vegetables. One favorite is sweet corn. Most farmers don't have many problems with raccoon damage because raccoons don't prefer wide-open farmland spaces. They prefer the forests or the protections offered in dense urban areas. If you decide to grow sweet corn in town there are a few things that may work. Grow it close to the house or grow shorter varieties that can be grown in containers—how attractive that could be in your edible landscape.

You may also consider growing the "three sisters." This is a specific group of plants that work together to enable each other to grow better. It was (and still is) a common way that some Native Americans grew food in the dry Southwest. Corn is planted. As it begins to grow well, you plant pole beans near the corn. The pole beans use the corn as a trellis and fix nitrogen on their root nodules for release as the roots die, releasing nitrogen to feed their neighbors. Corn is a wind-pollinated plant so plant it in blocks or groups, not long rows. The final sister is squash. Plant the squash in hills around the corn as you would normally plant it in your garden. The big leaves cover the soil and keep out most weed crops. The leaves mulch the growing area, keeping the soil moist and mitigating big temperature changes in the soil. The rough leaves also provide some protection from squirrels and raccoons, as these animals may not want to battle the prickly jungle to get to the sweet corn. That is the idea anyway, but urban critters can be persistent.

Raccoons can also be found raiding our ornamental ponds and eating the goldfish or expensive koi. You can protect the fish with the design of your water feature. Make sure the fish have a ledge to hide under and away from raccoon paws. This can be at the deep end of the feature as the raccoons generally will not jump into the water to get the fish. Covering the surface with deer netting may slow the raccoons and cause them to look elsewhere for food. Doing so also saves your fish from herons and other fishing birds.

Raccoons have a sensitive sense of smell so repellents may work well—those containing rotten eggs seem to work well to repel most raccoons. Remember to change them up, perhaps monthly. Again read, understand, and follow all label instructions. Not all repellents can be used on food crops so be careful where and when you use them.

Hot pepper sprays on plants being eaten will have some effect too. This does not mean the animal realizes all these plants taste awful. Some will continue to take bites of each plant because they do not see the connection. Of course, only use as directed. Reapply these repellents after heavy rains or watering or if temperatures melt them off the plants. Many are less effective in cold weather and may need to be reapplied more often.

RATS

Finding rats in your yard or home can be devastating. Black, or rooftop, rats are found mostly in attics, walls, trees, and shrubs. Brown (Norwegian) rats are found in basements, sewers, and in burrows alongside foundations.

Black rats (top) and Norway rats (bottom) are both common pests, but the two species typically target different areas of your house and yard.

You want to get rid of rats. They can carry diseases. They are omnivores and will, and do, eat just about everything. They can make a big impact on food stores or seeds, if left open and available for the rats to eat. Black rats tend to eat seeds, nuts, and berries while brown rats tend to eat grains. You will find rat droppings or see them or find their nests.

Call a professional if you wish, but there are some things you need to do unless you want another infestation. Clean away all debris—sanitation is key. Thin vegetation. Remove vines. Put pet food away at night and store all pet food, people food, and birdseed in pest-proof containers. Seal all entrances larger than ¼ inch. Keep screens and windows sealed tightly and in good repair. This goes for doors too.

Rats are bigger than mice. They can be found on all continents except Antarctica. They are adaptable. They live and exist well with humans and even seem to thrive living in our midst. They live only about one year but can multiply quickly. A rat's eyesight is not good, but its senses of hearing and smell are very good. Repellents may work for a short time but, again, remember rats are adaptable and they will adjust.

If you use traps, snap traps are a good choice. Glue boards may or may not work and they don't kill the animals. The animal suffers until it dies or you have to kill it. The snap traps will kill the animals instantly. Place the snap traps with bait along walls (for brown rats) or along walkways (for black rats)

Vines can look charming on the side of a house, but they are also an invitation for rats.

without setting them. Use lots of traps all at once. When the bait is taken, bait the traps again and set them. This will kill many rats at one time and limit the number of rats who are now trap shy.

Cats, dogs, owls, and hawks may be some of their predators but they usually cannot keep ahead of the population.

Using poisons is an option, but a dead rat in an area that you can't reach can be quite smelly. Plus, not all poisons act immediately so the poisoned rat may wander away and be eaten by one of your pets or by a predator and could eventually kill that pet or predator.

MICE

Mice can be found everywhere, in nearly every landscape, and you may only see them if they come into your home. Close small entrances so they can't get inside, and remove cover (such as tall grasses

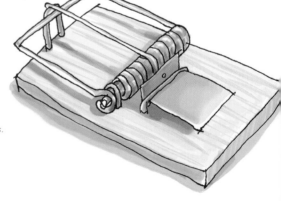

If you must use lethal traps for rats and mice, snap traps are generally much more humane than glue traps.

and heavy shrubbery) near your foundation, as they don't like to be in open spaces. (This strategy also discourages insects from coming into our homes in the cooler weather, as discussed on pages 74 and 75.) Mice eat many of the seeds from your bird feeder during the night, so feed only enough birdseed that will be eaten in full each day. Don't leave pet food out at night.

I find that chickens love to eat the mice that get into their run, but of course not everyone has mouse-catching chickens; repellents work in their place. Strong-smelling repellents, such as mint and citrus, seem to work very well to deter mice. Remember to switch the repellents frequently. Mice and voles may nibble on tender tree trunks and shrubs during winter so protect these with cylinders of hardware cloth.

Encourage raptors and owls into your landscape. Adding a few more open areas or places for owls to live or perch may mean these birds keep the mice population down. Hawks will help during the day.

Raptors are natural predators of rodents, so making your yard welcoming to them will help keep rat and mouse populations in check naturally.

SKUNKS

Skunks are nocturnal, but their black-and-white coloration is clear even in the dark. Nature colors animals black and white to warn predators that this may be one animal not to mess with and these animals are, as most of us know, equipped with quite a defensive weapon—the pungent spray they can expel with force from anal glands if they feel cornered or threatened.

If you, your dog, or your cat has been sprayed, the Humane Society of the United States suggests a bath made from 1 quart of 3 percent hydrogen peroxide (from any pharmacy), ¼ cup baking soda, and 1 teaspoon dishwashing liquid to combat the smell.

Avoid contact with this animal if at all possible, which is usually easy because they are crepuscular—active mostly from dusk until dawn. They are shy creatures that amble slowly. They don't climb well and want to avoid people whenever necessary. During the day they spend most of their time in their burrows.

Skunks may also be rabies carriers so, again, avoid contact when you can. Keep pets inside overnight and don't encourage skunks to feed in your yard by providing extra food for them. Clean away food scraps, bring pet food in at night, clean the grill, keep garbage cans covered, and, if needed, spray their outsides with repellents.

Skunks are solitary creatures and have small territories, which may overlap a bit. Mating takes place in late winter with males traveling through territories. This is also the time when many are killed on our roads. As for predators, skunks have only a few, including the great horned and barred owls along with coyotes, bobcats, cougars, dogs, and people. Cars, while not really predators, do account for many skunk deaths.

Skunks are omnivores. They prefer insects and grubs, which means they have strong claws for digging, and will make round holes in turf searching for grubs. This is good for the grass roots and may cause the death of many Japanese beetle grubs or larvae. If the damage appears overnight it may be from skunks. They will also eat frogs and snakes, including rattlesnakes. They eat crickets and beetles, including adult Japanese beetles. They also eat moles, eggs, lizards, and earthworms. This will be their spring and summer diet, along with carrion they find—dead birds and such. They also eat fungi (mushrooms) and seeds. In fall, they turn to higher-calorie and carbohydrate foods such as nuts, berries, and fruit. Skunks change their eating patterns to higher-calorie foods in fall because although they do not truly hibernate, they do enter a state of torpor, or sleep-like state, during winter months and need to build up their fat stores. They are seldom active in winter.

Round holes in your lawn are very likely the work of a skunk looking for grubs.

If you keep bees, keep your hives off the ground and out of the reach of skunks.

Skunks may also eat honeybees and wasps. If you have beehives, get them up off the ground. As skunks don't climb well, they will not climb up to the hives in most cases.

They are short-lived animals, living only one to three years in the wild. If you are dealing with a skunk problem, it may not be a long-lived one.

One reason so many skunks die on the roads is they do not have good vision—but they do have a good sense of smell and good hearing.

Depending on the time of year you may not really have a skunk problem. If they eat insects most of the year, they likely do not damage your plants. You may have to close the holes in the turf and replant a few dislodged plants. During fall, clean away fallen fruit and acorns, take in the bird feeder at night, and fill them only with enough seeds to be eaten each day. Consider adding hot pepper flakes to the birdseed you do put out—the skunks will probably not enjoy these seeds on the ground.

Skunks are good swimmers so they may enjoy a dip in your water feature. Make sure any fish have a safe spot to hide or put a cover of deer netting over the water feature. Skunks usually will live a mile or two from a water source, so if there is no open water near you—at all—you probably will not have a skunk in the neighborhood.

These are forest animals and prefer the protection of shrubs and brambles. Clean your yard of these items and the area will be less welcoming. While they do live in burrows, they can also live in woodpiles. Remove these, carefully, if you suspect a skunk resides there. Removing some of their cover and removing the

If skunks or other water-inclined animals are disturbing your pond, you can keep them out by covering it with netting.

wood pile they are living in will usually cause them to leave the area for less disturbed spaces. Adding some lights to your landscape may help them also to move on to a less well-lit area.

MOLES

These creatures are kind of funny looking but are quite good at removing grubs, worms, and other ground insects from our landscapes. A single mole may dig 200 to 500 feet in one night, so if you have lots of tunnels, it is probably just one mole. Think of it as a deep lawn aeration. Yes, some grass may die and you may have some tunnels you need to flatten, but, if you can, allow the mole to rid your lawn of the grubs. Once the insects are gone, the mole will move on. You can use repellents such as store-bought formulas with castor oil as their main component, with some success to convince the mole to move on sooner. Products that use vibrations will probably not work well—remember, moles are used to the vibrations we and our pets make walking around, and from cars driving by. Repair the lawn after the mole is gone.

VOLES

Voles are often confused with moles but are quite different. Voles are vegetarians, and while they do have tunnels underground they will often be spotted above ground. Moles are meat eaters and live mostly underground. They look quite different. The voles are similar to field mice in appearance and can cause a lot of damage in our gardens. Make your garden more inviting for foxes, hawks, owls, and eagles, which can help control the rodent population in your yard (see Chapter 4). Clean up tall grasses and feed birds only what will be eaten that day. When putting down winter mulches, make sure the ground is frozen, or nearly so, before you do. Otherwise, voles can live very well under the mulch on the plant roots in your garden all winter long. During the summer, voles will be eating seeds and will not cause as much damage—it is during the winter months while they are active underground eating plant roots when most of the damage occurs. They don't like wide-open spaces, so leave spaces around your gardens so that they have to travel a bit to get there. Visit your gardens frequently so that your presence is obvious to the voles. Repellents may work so try them also, remembering to change them up every few weeks. Make sure that all fallen fruit is cleaned up and you harvest your vegetable garden produce frequently.

OPOSSUMS

This ancient species was around when dinosaurs roamed the land. Opossums are nocturnal, active mostly at night. However, in winter or during times when food is less available, they may be active during daylight hours.

Possums are omnivores, meaning they eat a wide variety of food including insects, cockroaches, crickets, slugs, snails, frogs, small rodents, eggs, rotten fruit, rats, carrion (dead animals), garbage, and even ticks. They have been found to have ticks on them but, while grooming themselves, ingest the ticks, thus reducing tick populations where they are found. They do not seem to carry many of the tick diseases, either.

They will eat garbage left out, so keep areas around your trash cans clean. Remove food scraps after grilling and

Opossums are mostly nocturnal, but when food is scarce during the winter months, you are likely to see them during the day.

Baffle

bring pet food inside during the night. By removing many food sources, you reduce the chances that opossums will even consider your yard as a buffet. That said, they do enjoy slugs and you may thank the opossum if it clears your hosta bed of them.

The opossum is mostly found ambling slowly on the ground, but they can climb well. To prevent them from climbing to get bird food, remove the feeders at night or install squirrel baffles or large-diameter smooth plastic casings over the feeder's support pole. The opossum cannot grip the smooth large diameter and will not be able to climb. They do not hang by their prehensile tail, but do use it for balance on branches while climbing. That tail may also be used to hold nesting material.

An opossum's front paws are very dexterous. They can open latches and work out how to open other simple closures. They are gentle creatures that prefer quiet areas and will usually not present aggressive behavior and will slowly leave the area if confronted. I have found them trying to nest in the hen house; one was aggressive toward the chickens and I found the second one, quickly, before any damage was done to the birds and convinced it to leave the area, albeit slowly.

Baffles help deter squirrels, opossums, and other climbers from your birdfeeders.

These animals are short lived, living only one to two years in the wild. They have many natural predators, such as large owls, dogs, cats, humans, coyotes, bobcats, and raccoons, but these are not found in urban areas as we have removed them. Due to their eating carrion, many are killed while on the side of the road or crossing the roads.

They seldom use one den or sleeping place long, moving on to avoid predators. They are also wanderers by nature and so may not remain in your area long. They are solitary.

If one has denned up under a porch, set a board or fence against the area without initially securing it place—the animal will push it out or aside to get out and will probably not disturb the cover to get back in again. As soon as the cover has been disturbed, put it back in place. Check this cover every day for a few days—opossums are usually solitary, but a mother may have her young with her, and it is always possible that more than one animal may be in the same space, although this is rare. Once your cover goes for several days without being disturbed, this should mean that all the animals have left, and you can put a permanent barrier on the opening. Hardware cloth or chicken wire works well.

You can also try a flashing or strobe light in the area it calls home. Because they are shy creatures, preferring dark, safe areas, they will probably leave quickly.

WOODCHUCKS

Woodchucks—otherwise known as groundhogs or whistlepigs—can be a problem in our gardens due to the digging they do. Usually, an individual woodchuck will stay close to its burrow, seldom moving more than half a mile away. The burrow can be very long and can go deep, so trying to close them can be an issue. The main entrance will be marked by a larger pile of dirt, while smaller entrances, exits, and spyholes will be harder to spot. The openings may pose a threat to humans or larger animals walking in the area and falling into or tripping over them. These burrows aerate your soils and, during rain events or snowmelt, funnel the water from your property back to the water table or aquifer in your area. An abandoned woodchuck burrow may also become a home for a number of other animals, such as opossums, skunks, gophers, foxes, and snakes.

Woodchucks are little—or not so little—eating machines. They forage all day long, nibbling on seeds, small plants, and their favorite—clover. They avoid much activity during the heat of the day. I often see woodchucks on the local highway's shoulders. They don't see very well and this may account for the number hit by cars each year.

Because a woodchuck can live for two to seven years, this could be a problem for the homeowner. Woodchucks are creatures of habit. If you can dissuade them from their regular rounds they may

The main entrance to a woodchuck burrow can be identified by the pile of dirt near the entrance.

move on or ignore your favorite vegetable garden bed. They are solitary, so you generally only need to deal with one animal in your outdoor space—they don't like to share their territory. You can use this to help them move on.

Because woodchucks are prey animals, sprinkling blood meal around the areas you wish to protect or on their paths may cause them to leave. Also try repellents that work using strong smells, such as garlic or rotten eggs. Plant clover in your lawn to convince them to enjoy that area rather than the garden. Woodchucks do hibernate during winter months so they will not damage your trees or shrubs at that time. Being actively out in your yard and garden frequently makes it less hospitable to the woodchuck as it likes its quiet.

If you decide to close the burrows, make sure there are no young there—so do not do this in early spring to early summer. Do not wait too late in the year either as they do need time to find another place to live. Gently and loosely cover the main entrance of the burrow and all the small entrances too and wait three to five days to make sure the entrance is not cleared of the debris or disturbed. If there is no disturbance, seal it with hardware cloth and more soil. If you see digging elsewhere, proactively fill these places in loosely. Eventually, the woodchuck should move on to a quieter area with more amenable neighbors.

BIRDS

Birdwatching is the second most popular hobby in America today, closely following gardening. The two seem to go well together and, for the most part, they do. It is only when we lose our harvest or crops to birds do we get a little upset. Birds are an important part of our outdoor experience. We love to hear the spring calls of the cardinals as they declare territory or search for a mate. The chick-a-dee-dee call of chickadees can brighten any winter day. The colorful flash of a bluebird or oriole in our yards brings a smile to our face and the shadow of a hawk or eagle overhead helps us touch that wild, free part of our souls we sometimes lose touch with. But when the starlings eat all the carefully planted seeds in the garden, or the sparrows nest in our hanging baskets, destroying the plants, or the robins eat the cherries or serviceberries faster than we can imagine, we tend to get upset.

Planting both early- and late-blooming cherry trees in your yard helps ensure there is still fruit left for you.

Invite the birds into your yard with bird feeders and water—with birdbaths or ponds. Don't forget shrubs and trees for them to nest in. Allow some dead trees to remain, if they are safe and it is legal in your city—these are great places for those hawks, owls, and eagles to perch while they decide which "pest" critters to eat first.

Those starlings eating the seeds? They would love to help you by eating slugs from the hosta bed or Japanese beetles on the apple tree. The robins downing those cherries would love to feed all those pesky caterpillars that bother you to their chicks. The sparrows that sometimes nest in hanging baskets are sure to eat a lot of weed seeds before they sprout and create more work for you. So, it is just a matter of redirecting the bad behavior, or preventing it—or even learning to live with it.

Plant two kinds of cherry trees, one that fruits a bit early and one that fruits later. The birds will probably get the early ones, but leave the later-ripening ones for you. Understand that with the cherry trees or serviceberries you may lose the fruit on the upper branches but, if you are fast, you can get some from the lower branches.

Yes, the goldfinches will probably decimate your swiss chard. So, plant a garden area of swiss chard just for them and enjoy their antics as they dip and dive and fill the garden with bright yellow flashes of color. Cover the swiss chard you want to protect with floating row covers and your crop is safe!

Floating row covers can work also well in your vegetable garden to protect those newly planted seeds until they sprout and it can cover branches of the cherry or apple tree to protect the fruit you want to keep for yourself. Bagging your apples will help too (see pages 89 and 90).

To prevent birds from nesting in hanging baskets, set out the baskets after nesting season is well on its way. It is illegal to destroy almost all nests. It is cruel to destroy them once eggs have been laid or young have hatched. Purchase your baskets—even ones that aren't as full or draping yet—and use them as container plants for a few weeks. You may be able to save money by purchasing less full baskets and, because you won't display them for a few weeks, they have time to fill out. Once the birds find other more acceptable places to nest, you can hang your now-well-growing baskets. And the containers you had them in? Time to grow more plants in them! A new look for the same area—maybe even start some vegetables in the containers for a totally different approach to container gardening.

If you don't want to wait to display the hanging containers, cover them with bird netting for a short time. If you do this, check the basket and netting frequently, many times a day, in case a bird becomes stuck there. You surely do not want a bird to die a slow and painful death trapped and without escape. Another tactic that may work is to install many upright sticks in the basket so it is uncomfortable and, perhaps, too tight for the birds to find a spot to construct the nest. You could even set out a sacrificial hanging basket—once the birds set up housekeeping, carefully move it to a more suitable place. Make sure it is a place similar to the original location and the parent birds see you doing it. Be prepared: they will not be happy with your action.

Are birds pecking the tomatoes? They could be testing to see whether those tomatoes are ripe apples or they could be chasing bugs on them—or they could just be interested. Needless to say, that pecking can leave little marks and bruises on your tomatoes. Don't remove too many leaves from the tomatoes; let them hide some of the crop. Floating row covers over tomato plants work too, or try different colors of tulle and really "fancy up" your garden—this may be only for the really adventurous or artistic.

Floating row covers protect freshly planted seeds from birds—not to mention protecting young plants from rabbits and other pests until the plants are established.

I think every outdoor space can only become more special when a plethora of birds inhabits it. They add life and movement and sound to our yards and gardens. Because the birds eat so many caterpillars, beetles, insects, and weed seeds, any damage they do seems far outweighed by the benefits they bring to our yards.

If you plan carefully, you can even entice migrating birds to stop and enjoy sustenance so they continue their migration fully fueled. Research your favorite migrating birds and figure out how to encourage these speedy visitors to stop in and grace your outdoor space for a short time. For example, keep the hummingbird feeders filled until you know the last have migrated through. Leave your ornamental grasses up and your flowers that have gone to seed, as birds may avail themselves of the seeds you have left for them. Keep your feeders and birdbaths filled. If possible, reduce your outdoor lighting during migration times—birds often migrate at night, and light pollution can confuse them.

If you live in an area with harsh winters, include some trees with persistent fruit that will feed the birds in winter. Water in winter is another winner to invite the birds in, as are feeders. These all allow you to watch life flourishing in your yard in the dead of winter while you are safe and warm inside.

If your area is prone to droughts, keep the water containers filled. If heavy rains are frequent, include areas for shelter from the downpours.

ORGANIC AND HUMANE CONTROL FOR PETS AND HUMAN PESTS

7

We want our dogs and cats to be safe in our yards. To do this, we may need to fence the yard to keep the dog in and, when outside, put our cat on a leash.

DOGS

If you have dogs, there are some plants you should keep them away from, such as grapes and daylilies—both are poisonous for your dog. For cats, one of the deadliest plants is the Easter lily.

If you find your dog being a pest in your yard, figure out what behavior is causing the problem. Is your dog digging? Provide a sand pit where the dog can dig to his heart's content. Add a toy or two for him to bury and then rediscover.

If you find that dog spots in the grass are an issue, consider that dogs and grass are not a good combination. Basically, your dog's urine overfertilizes, or burns, the grass. As soon as your dog pees, flush the area with water to dilute the fertilizer. Or train your dog to do her business in one particular area. This may be easier with male dogs if you give them a spot to aim for—so install a pee rock or pee post and let your dog use that. Praise him every time he uses that area. Use only positive reinforcement and soon he may only use that rock or post. Female dogs can be similarly trained to use a particular

area of mulch or gravel. The scent of past events reinforces the continued use of the same area. Some dogs need privacy to do their business; respect that and add a small shrub, fence, or other barrier that will allow the privacy and yet still blend with your landscape plan. In fact, the fence or shrub may enhance your landscape if you place it properly. The hidden "dog area" can be a secret you and your dog keep from almost everyone. Limiting elimination spots means you can now grow a nice lawn and also not have to pick up dog feces all over your yard. If you have children, that may mean they are free to run everywhere else in the yard.

When landscaping with a dog (or dogs) in mind, there are some things to consider. Most dogs like to patrol the area. They will have a path of patrol they will take each time they reenter their yard. Allow this. Don't plant in these areas. Just add mulch or gravel paths. If you have a fence, make sure your dog can see through parts of it. This enables her to keep watch and protect her territory. A dog that can't see at all beyond the fence is more likely to keep barking at everything or become more aggressive to anything outside the fence.

Your dog will also want a running path. Allow it and plant to the sides of these paths. When installing plants, consider size. Let the plants be large enough to impress your dog. He will respect plants that reach chest level or taller. Masses of plants will be seen as a big wall rather than a few plants here and there that will be ignored and run right over. If your dog spends much time out in the yard, make sure he can't get out; make sure he has shade and water, and, if on a chain or leash, that he can't get hung up in bushes or shrubs or even jump over a fence partway while still on the chain.

Dogs are pack animals and most want to be a part of *your* pack. Some dogs are guard or herd dogs. That is their job—to guard their pack or their herd. Give your dog a job to do and he will be less bored and less likely to get into trouble. It is up to you, the human, to know what job she can do. Most breeds were bred for some specific purpose. That may give you some direction in deciding what job your dog needs.

If other dogs entering your yard are the pests, find the owners and request they control their animals. If dog walkers often pass your yard, you may find that, while they clean up well after their pets, urine is still a problem with some of your plants. As for your dog, install a pee post or rock if legal to do so and you're so inclined. Put up a funny sign: "doggy social network," "doggy texting area," or whatever works for you. You can also add mulch around the area to encourage all the elimination to take place in one area of your yard. If you find dogs running free, most cities and towns have leash laws and you will do the runaway dog a favor by reporting it. The animal could be hit by a car or attacked by a very aggressive dog.

CATS

If you have a cat you allow out on the leash, make sure you are always out there with her. A cat tied up on a leash is easy prey for a dog who hates cats or even a large eagle. You must keep the cat safe. Even if he still has claws, he will not be able to protect himself from a dog or eagle attack.

If you decide to plant catnip for your cat but other cats in the neighborhood seem to destroy it before you are able to share it with your feline friend, try planting from seeds rather than putting in a young plant; the seeds do not release the essential oils that attract cats. Plant the herb away from the walkway so you won't brush against it and release the essential oils that excite the cats.

Catmint and catnip are a nice garden treat for your felines—
but if you plant it, be aware that feral cats like it too.

If other cats use your yard as a litter box, consult the animal control laws in your town or city. Many people think it is fine to let their cat roam free. They don't realize they put their pet in danger of being hit by a car or attacked by a dog or wild animal. Plus, cats take and kill wild songbirds, many of which are endangered and all of which are protected species. If you feel comfortable confronting the owner, politely advise him of the law and the protected species his pet is killing. If you don't feel comfortable with this, contact animal control or just make your yard unwelcoming to neighborhood cats.

If they use part of your garden for a litter box or to sunbathe, plant a number of 6- to 10-inch-long sticks in the open soil so the cats can't lay down or rake the soil easily with their claws. Pinecones may work as an uncomfortable mulch. Repellents may work—cats seem to dislike the smell of citrus. Some cats also dislike the smell of rue but, for some, it is a challenge and they resort to spraying the plant when they can. A motion-activated scarecrow that sprays water when activated may also work on cats, and even dogs, in your yard without permission.

HUMANS

Yes, even humans can be pests in your garden. It may be deliberate, like that person taking your fresh tomatoes right before you harvest them, or unintentional, like the children who take a shortcut through your yard or accidentally stomp through your garden while they are playing.

If people are the pests in your landscape, you may need to do a number of things. A fence is a good start, but not just any fence. Tall wooden fences may be your first thought. Remember, though, if safety is your goal, that if you cannot see out, no one can see in either. If someone is in your yard or breaking into your home and the backyard is all fenced in with tall fences, no one will see what is happening. So, shorter fences or even chain-link or iron fences may be your best bet. Enlist your neighbors to build a community and watch over each other. This is often the best defense. Build your neighborhood. Know who belongs there or who is visiting.

Consider a **DO NOT ENTER** or no trespassing sign. These won't stop a determined troublemaker but may make others think twice. The sign can be obvious without being obnoxious.

Plant your vegetable garden where you can harvest from it frequently, and avoid planting in your front yard unless you don't mind some of your veggies going missing— the best result would be children raiding the garden for fresh food and eating it and enjoying it. If you have a patio out in public this may not be the best place for those pots of tomato plants. Place your very valuable plants or statuary in

Stinging nettles, raspberries, or other plants with thorns or spines keep human pests away from your vegetable garden.

a more protected part of your yard. Make sure that there are borders to your gardens or planting beds. Mown grass, rock borders, and short, decorative fences all show that this is a planned, cared-for area. These kinds of areas are more likely to be respected by someone just moving past or through your space.

One of the best deterrents to problems is to be visible and connected, so it helps to be seen frequently in your garden. When people walk by, say hello and engage them in a quick discussion. It is less likely for people to cause problems in your yard if they know you.

Sometimes the problem is children who either don't understand boundaries, are into mischief, or are just having too much innocent fun to consider they are trespassing. Fences will help, as will knowing their names. Once you are a friend, they will think twice about entering your garden without permission. If you share open front yards with your neighbors as part of your neighborhood culture, you need to buy into the neighborhood you have chosen to live in. Work with your neighbors to come up with solutions.

Should you need or want to redirect traffic around a corner in your yard or away from a secluded area such as behind or between garages, plant raspberries, roses, or stinging nettles. All are uncomfortable plants to deal with unexpectedly, yet none will really harm anyone. The raspberries provide fruit, the roses give flowers, and the stinging nettle makes a great spring green or tea later on. It is also a nice caterpillar food plant for some butterflies.

Motion-activated water sprinklers can be effective deterrents. You may even want to install one in the front yard. Turn it on during a hot day and let the children cool off while running through the water. The kids will love it. Make sure their parents are okay with it. And you may even make friends with those you considered pests in the past. After all, it is simply a matter of how you view things.

CONCLUSION

Our world is filled with a wide variety of animals and insects, many of which impact our outdoor spaces. Sometimes we encourage and welcome these impacts, as by feeding the birds or planting flowers for pollinators. Other times it seems like these animals and insects are out to destroy our carefully planted spaces despite our best-laid plans.

By thinking from the perspective of the animal or insect, we can perceive our world through their eyes and noses. We may find that once we change our point of view, we can see why our landscape is so attractive to that pest. In this way, we can change what we plant or how we manage our outdoor space to limit the "bad" interactions and increase the "good" interactions with our fellow inhabitants. Sometimes we may just have to live with the animals or insects and their impacts; other times we will be able to influence what occurs.

As our climate changes, we will encounter new animals and insects. Because we have learned to deal with the current visitors to our outdoor spaces, we can use this knowledge to make dealing with new challenges much more easily. All animals and insects simply want to find food and a safe place to live and raise their young. That is not always what we want to happen in our landscapes so changes can be made to make our outdoor spaces welcoming to us, but less welcoming to the pests we want to avoid.

Once we have learned and applied the basic concepts of healthy yard and garden management and instigated safe and humane pest controls and made them a part of our lives, we may find that we enjoy our connect with nature even more as we employ less work on our part and get more satisfaction in return.

When our landscapes are healthy and diverse, we find that no one pest is too much in evidence. Nature seems to control and balance many of the problems that we encounter, and we can work with nature to make that happen. When we see our outdoor living space as a whole system rather than simply one small space after another, we can view the big picture and see how all the small fragments influence the health and vitality of the whole. If we insist on growing only one thing then we know that we will be inviting nature's response to that bounty. We can anticipate nature's reaction to the changes we make in our landscapes.

APPENDIX

PEST CONTROL AT A GLANCE

INSECTS

PEST	SOLUTIONS	MORE INFORMATION
Aphids	• Encourage or introduce ladybugs in your garden • Treat moderate aphid problems with a strong stream of water • Treat more serious infestations with insecticidal soap	pages 86-88
Apple Maggot Flies	• Red sticky traps • Kaolin clay spray • Fruit-tree insecticidal sprays • Bag your apples	pages 88-90
Four-Lined Plant Bugs	• Spray nymphs with insecticidal soap • Squish adults • Remove aboveground parts of affected plants at end of growing season	pages 90-91
Japanese Beetles	• Encourage predatory bird populations • Protect vulnerable plants with floating row covers • Remove emerging scouts early in the morning • Avoid Japanese beetle traps except at the edge of your yard and only in cases of high populations • If pesticides are needed, apply in mid to late summer	pages 84-86
Leafminers	• Remove affected leaves and dispose of properly	page 90
Sawflies	• Young larvae: remove from plants with a strong stream of water or pick off by hand • Larvae larger than 1': spray with insecticidal soap	pages 81-82
Scale	• Encourage predatory bird populations • Spray young crawlers with insecticidal soap • Pry off or apply rubbing alcohol to hardened adults • As last resort, use systemic pesticide	pages 91-92
Spittlebugs	• Take no action unless populations are high • If needed, remove with a strong stream of water	page 84
Squash Vine Borers	• Delay squash planting • Protect young plants with floating row covers • Remove borers from affected plants and rebury stems	pages 92-93

ANIMALS

PEST	SOLUTIONS	MORE INFORMATION
Birds	• Protect vulnerable plants with floating row covers • Bag apples on apple trees • Cover hanging baskets with netting, install upright sticks, or wait to hang until nesting season is already underway	pages 122-125
Chipmunks	• Cover newly planted seed rows with hardware cloth • Use predator urine, blood meal, or strong-smelling scent repellants such as garlic, rotten eggs, or spices • Use hot pepper sprays as a taste deterrent • Add hot pepper flakes to birdseed to discourage feeding • Reduce areas of cover • Encourage predatory bird populations	pages 97-99
Deer	• Install fencing or deer netting at yard entry points • Plant hedgerows or thorny plants as barriers • Protect young plants with bird netting • Use predator urine or strong-smelling scent repellents • Use sound and visual repellants • Install motion-activated lighting or sprinklers • Place deer-attracting plants closer to your house or surround them with ornamental grasses or fragrant herbs • Protect vulnerable tree trunks with hardware cloth • Protect evergreens with deer fencing in winter • Don't leave fruit, acorns, or birdseed on the ground	pages 103-108
Gophers	• Install fencing that extends at least 2' into the ground • Protect vulnerable plants with wire baskets • Remove cover and encourage human traffic near tunnel entrances • Humanely trap and remove animals • Encourage predatory bird populations	page 100
Mice	• Clean up fallen seeds, nuts, and berries • Remove vines and cover near homes • Seal all entrances larger than ¼" and keep screens and windows sealed tightly • Use citrus, mint, or other scent repellents • Protect vulnerable tree trunks and shrubs with hardware cloth • Encourage predatory bird populations	pages 114-115
Moles	• Use castor oil repellents • If possible, wait for the moles to exhaust your grub population and move on of their own accord	page 118
Opossums	• Keep outdoor garbage areas clean and secure • Use birdfeeders with baffles or other physical barriers • Block off possible hiding areas, such as under porches • Install motion-activated lighting	pages 119-121
Rabbits	• Install rabbit fencing as soon as you plant • Surround more vulnerable plants with thickly planted herbs or other strong-smelling or strong-tasting plants • Plant clover to distract from other attractive plants • Apply blood meal, predator urine, or synthetic repellent • Protect vulnerable tree trunks with hardware cloth • Block off possible hiding areas, such as under porches	pages 95-97

ANIMALS

PEST	SOLUTIONS	MORE INFORMATION
Raccoons	• Keep outdoor garbage areas clean and secure • Clean up fallen fruit and birdseed • Remove tree limbs that may allow access to your home • Use strong-smelling scent repellants or hot pepper sprays • Install motion-activated lighting or sprinklers • Install loose, bendable fencing that cannot be climbed easily • Clean and disinfect areas noticeably used by raccoons • Place attractive plants close to your house • Cover ponds with deer netting	pages 106-112
Rats	• Clean up fallen seeds, nuts, and berries • Remove vines and cover near homes • Seal all entrances larger than ¼" and keep screens and windows sealed tightly	pages 112-118
Skunks	• Keep outdoor garbage areas clean and secure • Keep beehives off the ground • Clean up fallen seeds, nuts, berries, and fruit • Clean outdoor grills after using • Use scent repellents to disguise food smells • Add hot pepper flakes to birdseed to discourage feeding • Minimize protective bushes and other cover	pages 115-118
Squirrels	• Apply mulch over freshly dug soil to disguise the scent • Use scent repellents on plant bulbs • Add hot pepper flakes to birdseed to discourage feeding • Use birdfeeders with baffles or other physical barriers • Provide water sources to discourage feeding on tomatoes and other fruit • Bag apples on apple trees	pages 100-102
Voles	• Protect vulnerable tree trunks with hardware cloth • Clean up fallen birdseed and tall grasses • Leave open spaces between garden plots • Encourage fox, hawk, owl, and eagle populations	pages 118-119
Woodchucks	• Use blood meal or strong-smelling scent repellents • Plant clover to distract from other attractive plants • Close up empty burrows	pages 121-122

RESOURCES

CATALOGS

Baker Creek Heirloom
  Seeds
www.rareseeds.com
417.924.8917

Burpee
www.burpee.com
800.888.1447

Gardener's Supply
  Company
www.gardeners.com
888.833.1412

Gardens Alive!
www.gardensalive.com
513.354.1482

GrowOrganic.com
www.groworganic.com
888.784.1722

Gurney's Seed &
  Nursery Co.
www.gurneys.com
513.354.1492

JungSeed.com
www.jungseed.com
800.297.3123

Park Seed
www.parkseed.com
800.845.3369
Plow & Hearth
www.plowhearth.com
800.494.7544

Raintree Nursery
www.raintreenursery.com
800.391.8892

The Online Greenhouse
www.theonline
  greenhouse.com
860.782.1934

Seeds of Change
www.seedsofchange.com
888.762.7333

White Flower Farm
www.whiteflowerfarm.
  com
800.503.9624

PRODUCTS

Bonide
Critter, insect, and weed
  control products
www.bonide.com
315.736.8231

Deer No No
Nontoxic deer repellent
www.deernono.com
855.770.3820

Guardener
Solar-powered, pest-
  repelling devices
www.guardeners.com
301.628.7270

Havahart
Pest repellents, humane
  pest traps, and more
www.havahart.com
908.769.4242

Liquid Fence
Deer, rabbit, goose, mole,
  and snake repellents
www.liquidfence.com
800.917.5438

Plantskydd
Deer, rabbit, and elk
  repellents
www.plantskydd.com
604.885.3535

Repellex
Deer, rabbit, mole,
  gopher, and squirrel
  repellents
www.repellex.com
877.737.3539

Safer Brand
Insect control and lawn
  care
www.saferbrand.com
855.767.4264

ORGANIZATIONS

The Humane Society
www.humanesociety.org
866.720.2676

USDA Animal and Plant
  Health Inspection
  Service
www.aphis.usda.gov
844.820.2234

US Environmental
  Protection Agency
www.epa.gov

INDEX